Inside *The Scottish Kitchen*, you'll find a recipe for every meal and occasion, whether you're looking for a feast to feed the family on Burns Night or a piece of tablet or shortbread to enjoy with your tea. *The Scottish Kitchen* combines cherished family recipes passed down through generations with innovative new twists on beloved local favorites. Included are chapters on:

- Soups & Starters
- Comfort Food
- Haggis
- Fish & Shellfish
- Meat & Game
- Veggie & Vegan
- Baking & Desserts
- Wee Treats

From bustling cities to idyllic isles, this engrossing cookbook evokes one of the world's most beautiful countries and its cuisine on every page.

The Scottish Kitchen

Published in Canada by Appetite by Random House®,
a division of Penguin Random House Canada Limited.

www.penguinrandomhouse.ca

Appetite by Random House® and colophon are registered trademarks
of Penguin Random House LLC.

Library and Archives Canada Cataloguing in Publication is available upon request.

ISBN: 978-0-525-61270-4
eBook ISBN: 978-0-525-61271-1

Cover photography: Castle Stalker: RPH Foto / via Adobe Stock;
Salmon: shutterstock / Marian Weyo; Tartan: shutterstock / margit777
Book photography: Susie Lowe (except images listed on page 273)

Printed in China

10 9 8 7 6 5 4 3 2 1

appetite
by RANDOM HOUSE

Penguin
Random House
Canada

The Scottish Kitchen

More than 100
Timeless Traditional and
Contemporary Recipes
from Scotland

Gary Maclean

Food photography by Susie Lowe

appetite
by RANDOM HOUSE

For my wonderful wife, Sharon
and to our amazing children, who inspire us both –
Cameron, Ewan, Laura, Eilidh, Finlay and Harris

CONTENTS

FISH & SHELLFISH

MEAT & GAME

VEGGIE & VEGAN

BAKING & DESSERTS

WEE TREATS

INDEXES

CASTLE STALKER, ARGYLL

FOREWORD

BY SAM HEUGHAN

When I think of home, it's the food that springs to mind and always transports me back there. Of course, across the world people associate Scotland with haggis – our most well-known dish – but there's so much more to Scotland than that. There's the comfort of holding a warm Scotch pie in your hand on a blustery afternoon while watching a football match; the nostalgia of a hot plate of stovies or a homemade shepherd's pie; a spicy, soul-warming dram of whisky in front of the fire (perhaps my own Sassenach!); or the simple pleasure of haggis, neeps and tatties, our unofficial national dish. On every page of this book, I was transported back to Scotland.

For many years now, I've been passionate about bringing Scotland's heritage to the world stage through my own work, and this is also precisely what Gary does in *The Scottish Kitchen*. It's wonderful to see traditional Scottish food like venison, grouse, lobster and langoustines being enjoyed across the world now. Gary has worked tirelessly educating people all over the globe about our incredible produce and time-honoured traditions, and reinvigorating Scottish cuisine with his own inventions. Nobody knows Scottish food like Gary Maclean: as if winning *MasterChef: The Professionals* and collecting countless culinary awards wasn't enough, he was also named Scotland's first National Chef – and all of his knowledge and passion is now distilled in these pages.

Some of the recipes and traditions shared in this book go back hundreds of years, adapted and treasured by families who passed down their knowledge to their children, and their children's children – and now these recipes are in your hands. I hope you enjoy learning more about Scotland's history and culture through our food, and I'm thankful to Gary for sharing this with us. I can't wait for you to discover more of Scotland with him.

LUSKENTYRE, ISLE OF HARRIS

INTRODUCTION

INTRODUCTION

BY GARY MACLEAN

I have long been fascinated by the relationship between Scotland and North America. My love for all things North American-Scottish began over 25 years ago when I spent some time with the Chicago Scots, a not-for-profit organization that fosters Scottish culture throughout the city, doing a culinary demonstration for a fundraiser they held at Navy Pier. From that trip on, I have delved into the history and impact Scotland has had on North America. Did you know of the 46 men who have been President of the United States, 35 of them are of Scots decent? Or that the US Declaration of Independence was partly modeled on Scotland's 1320 Declaration of Arbroath? Or that 21 out of 56 men who signed the Declaration of Independence were of Scottish descent, and two of them were born in Scotland? Likewise, I was thrilled to discover that the first Prime Minister of Canada, John A. Macdonald, was born in my home city of Glasgow –I actually ran a restaurant just a few feet away from the plaque that marks his birthplace.

Other great Scots have not only impacted the US and Canada but also the world. Telephone inventor Alexander Graham Bell was born in Edinburgh in 1847. Steel magnate and philanthropist Andrew Carnegie was born in Dunfermline in 1835. Car manufacturer David Dunbar Buick was born in Arbroath in 1854. Uncle Sam, Davy Crockett, Mickey Mouse, George Washington, Neil Armstrong all links to Scotland. The Scottish influence in the birth of modern America was acknowledged in Senate Resolution 155 – 105th Congress (1997–1998), which declares April 6th each year to be designated and observed as National Tartan Day. The resolution honors the role, "that Scottish Americans played in the founding of the Nation". Now thousands of people from all over the US and Canada descend on New York City to celebrate all things Scottish and march up 6th Avenue in the annual Tartan Day parade.

As a chef, educator and food ambassador, I have been promoting Scottish food at home and abroad for over 30 years, serving the great and the good in the most wonderful locations all over the world and showcasing our produce and food traditions from Singapore to Los Angeles and everywhere in between. I have been lucky to work with amazing organizations all over the US and Canada, teaching at incredible culinary schools and making many friends along the way. And the more I travel, the prouder I become of my homeland.

I decided to write this book because I felt that a book celebrating Scottish traditional food, written for a modern kitchen and lifestyle, had not been done before. During the process of writing this book, I have learned loads myself about Scottish recipes and regional traditions, and found myself calling friends all over the country to ask about their childhood memories of food and to support me with any regional recipes I might have missed. I have tried to include every aspect of our food, from land and sea—not just from our past but recipes that are as relevant now as they have always been.

Scotland's larder has some of the world's most sought-after food. Its phenomenal beef, fish and shellfish are unrivaled – from langoustines to black puddings, from hot smoked salmon to Shetland mussels. With to-die-for flavor combinations, Scottish cooks have long known the pleasures of creating dishes that use superbly fresh, seasonal and locally-sourced produce. Scotland has been forged by centuries of influence from foreign lands, weather and a changing landscape, and this is reflected in the food Scots eat today.

Consider, for example, Scottish livestock. The Scottish climate lends itself to producing amazing lamb and beef: our wet weather and terrain provide ideal conditions for grazing animals, making them hardy and strong. Scotch beef ranks amongst the most renowned in the world, so much so that the word Angus is commonly used as a mark of quality. How much of this "Angus" beef served abroad is part of the famous breed is unclear, but the sheer hint that the breed has come from Scotland is enough for millions of consumers to pay a premium for it.

We are blessed with an incredible coastline of 11,000 kilometres around Scotland, if you include the islands; that's more coastline than France and Spain combined. The first settlers of Scotland did not take advantage of this magnificent bounty, preferring to live off the land and not the ocean. It was not until the 8th century, influenced by Norsemen, that we started to fish for commercial purposes. The Vikings arrived initially as pirates and marauders but returned to settle mainly in Shetland, Orkney and the Outer Hebrides, bringing with them boat-building and fishing skills. The biggest problem was that the catch was highly perishable. Various ways of preserving fish were developed, including drying, salting and smoking – traditions we still maintain today in Scotland. Staples like Arbroath smokies have stood the test of time, and cold smoked salmon has a global appeal.

We are now experts in aquaculture and annually export £640 million worth of farmed salmon across the globe. Our shellfish is also highly prized: Scotland is the leading European supplier of langoustine, which thrive in Scotland's cold seas and lochs. We produce over £80 million worth of langoustine a year, which are shipped both live and frozen to North America, Europe and Asia. Scottish lobster is also popular – it can be found on the menu in over 20 Michelin-starred restaurants in Tokyo alone.

During the 19th century, Scotland became a playground for the wealthy of the south. Every autumn the trains from London's Kings Cross station were filled with the guns and fishing rods of the industrial giants of the day, destined for the Highlands of Scotland, with forests and rivers teeming with life. Queen Victoria had an influence on all things Scottish. When she purchased the Balmoral estate, it opened the floodgates: Scotland became the place to be for the rich, helping to forge the shortbread-tin image of Scotland today. My own family history is tied into this amazing period: my great-great-grandfather was a gillie (a person who attends someone on a hunting or fishing expedition) on a Highland estate, and I also had relations who worked at Balmoral for Queen Victoria.

Historically, we have also had great choice in vegetables (regardless of misconceptions to the contrary), with the Edinburgh and Glasgow markets offering broccoli, peas, greens, potatoes, turnips, onions, cauliflower, asparagus and savoy cabbage. We also had a great many orchards dating as far back as the 13th century. Modern-day Scotland produces enough soft fruit to export and our seed potatoes are planted in farms all over the world. Some of our most famous food and drink contain crops like barley and oats: oats are a key ingredient in our famous haggis, and barley is vital in the making of whisky.

There is now also a food revolution going on in Scotland's inner-city cooperatives, which are bringing people together to grow vegetables in vacant, unused land. The Wash House Garden, an organic, no-dig market garden in Parkhead, Glasgow, provided a lot of the amazing produce used in this book. Commercially, the garden grows organic fruit and vegetables for sale and donation, giving local people access to some of the best food possible. By also hosting inherently fun and therapeutic workshops for all ages, community volunteering sessions, free meals and events, the organization provides opportunities for people to connect with good food, the natural world, themselves and one another. In so doing, it improoofs mental and physical well-being, builds skills and knowledge and brings people together – all while getting their hands dirty and filling their bellies!

My whole career I have been fascinated by the story of Scotland's traditional foods and, at the same time, enthralled by the ingenuity and creativity alive in Scotland today. I hope *The Scottish Kitchen* opens a small window into our world so that we can keep those traditions alive for generations to come.

HOW THIS BOOK WORKS

The first thing I want to say to you is chill out when cooking – it's only a plate of food. When cooking savory food, you have in many cases the ability to add, substitute or adapt what the recipe states. For example, if a recipe calls for 1lb (454g) of ground meat and your package is a bit more or a bit less, just use what you've got. Sweet recipes and most things with a combination of butter, flour and sugar need to be followed precisely.

Butter is always unsalted; it is much better for cooking with. In years gone by, the salted butter was cheaper, but nowadays they are more or less the same price.

I use two different **oils** throughout the book. When a recipe calls for good oil, it is up to you to choose a good-quality oil – either extra virgin olive oil or, as I prefer, cold-pressed canola oil, which is easily found in Scotland and North America. Cooking oil is exactly what it says: oil for cooking. This can be sunflower oil, vegetable oil, groundnut oil – it's up to you.

The oven temperatures are all fan-assisted, so if you do not have a fan-assisted oven, increase the temperature by about 10%, and follow the visual cues in the recipe to know when things are done.

I have included **measurements** in both imperial and metric so the recipes will be accessible to you wherever you live in the world.

PLOCKTON HARBOUR, THE HIGHLANDS

SOUPS & STARTERS

COCK-A-LEEKIE

When I was a young chef, cock-a-leekie was always a bit of a puzzle for me: the only time I ever saw it was at our Hogmanay or Burns Night banquets. The reason it was a puzzle was that I couldn't understand why we would add prunes to a perfectly nice chicken broth! This recipe is my version of cock-a-leekie – one I remember from my early days as a chef.

This broth has been made in Scotland for hundreds of years. It probably originated in France and changed to fit with what was available in Scotland. This recipe has rice, but you could use barley or oats.

MAKES 10 PORTIONS

1 small chicken

4 medium white onions, chopped

1 medium leek, chopped

2 celery sticks, chopped

4 sprigs of thyme

1 bay leaf

Scant 2 tablespoons (25ml) good oil

Generous 1/3 cup (85g) long grain rice, cooked

10 dried prunes, cut into strips

1 bunch of flat-leaf parsley, shredded

Salt and black pepper

This recipe can be easily made vegan if you use a good quality vegetable stock and replace the chicken with a meat-free alternative; it also speeds up the process as you won't have to cook it for so long.

1. Cock-a-leekie soup, for me, is a refined clear broth. You should be able to identify all the ingredients of the soup in your bowl. To do this, we need a very good stock. First, take your chicken and pop it into a large pot. Next, add half of your chopped onions, a handful of chopped leek, the chopped celery, thyme and bay leaf.

2. Cover with cold water and put onto the stovetop, then bring to the boil. Reduce the heat and simmer for 90 minutes, making sure you skim the broth and remove any scum that might come to the top.

3. Next remove the chicken from the pot and set aside. Strain the broth and discard the vegetables, but keep the stock.

4. Next, in a clean pot add your oil, the rest of the leeks and the remainder of your onion, and slowly cook until the onions soften.

5. Meanwhile, your chicken should have cooled enough that you can carefully remove the meat. Once done, you can chop it into smaller pieces.

6. When your onions are soft, stir in your chicken stock, the chopped chicken, cooked rice and the cut prunes.

7. Finish with the shredded parsley, and season with salt and a few good turns of black pepper.

CULLEN SKINK

Cullen skink is one of those recipes that is so easy to make and provides the biggest wow factor ever. The origins of Cullen skink go back to a small fishing village in the north-east of Scotland called Cullen. It has an incredible and well-documented history, with connections to King Robert the Bruce and Robert Burns. Skink is an old Scots word for shin or knuckle, and soups were often made from these cuts, hence it has developed the secondary meaning of a soup. So, in short, soup from Cullen.

I have made Cullen skink at lots of events around the world and people are amazed at its flavor. During a cooking demonstration I gave at the New Hampshire Highland Games, I said to more than 300 people that Cullen skink was better than their New England clam chowder. As you can imagine, this didn't go down too well with the local crowd. I had one trick up my sleeve, however, as I had prepared 300 taster portions of Cullen skink in the back for them to try. I don't think people could believe how good it was and they agreed it was better than the local chowder.

I often talk about soup being better the second day but this one is the exception: Cullen skink is best eaten straight away. If I have this on a restaurant menu, it is made twice a day – once for lunch, then again for dinner service–to make sure it's always fresh.

7oz (200g) pale smoked haddock

3 cups (750ml) whole milk

1 bay leaf

Scant 2 tablespoons (25g) butter

1 medium onion, finely diced

1lb (450g) potatoes, peeled and cut into ½in (1cm) cubes

Salt and pepper

1. Your first job when making Cullen skink is to flavor the milk. To do so, I use the trimmings from the haddock – with smoked haddock, you have to remove the center spine between the fillets, and there are also sometimes little bones around the edges of the fillets that need to be removed. Place the trimmings into a pot with the milk and the bay leaf, and put it on a low heat to simmer for a couple of minutes. This will really infuse the flavor from the smoky fish into the whole soup.

2. Dice the rest of the fish and set aside.

3. Next melt the butter in a large saucepan. Add the chopped onion and cook on medium heat for a few minutes without coloring, until soft.

4. Next add the diced potatoes, then strain the infused milk over the potatoes and the onion. Fish out the bay leaf from the strainer and add that to the pan as well.

5. Leave to cook for 15 to 20 minutes, until the potatoes are tender. You will actually see the milk thicken a little as the starch comes out of the potatoes.

6. Add the diced haddock and cook for no more than 5 minutes. Don't overcook the fish.

7. Double check the seasoning: I find most times the salt levels are good, as the haddock helps, but a few good turns of the pepper mill make all the difference.

DRESSED BROWN CRAB

Brown crab is amazing, and if you have never tried it you are missing out. Scotland's geography and weather are perfect for producing brown crab; we land thousands of tons every year and most of it is exported to Asia. Normally, I go for the biggest crabs I can find, but when you are preparing dressed crab it is always better to go smaller, as one crab is a portion. When I am in Oban, I head for the pier to the seafood restaurants and get a beautifully prepared dressed crab. Brown crabs are caught all around the coasts of Scotland – they are creel caught, the most sustainable type of fishing, which has very little impact on the seabed.

MAKES 1 CRAB

1x 1lb to 2lb (450g to 900g) live brown crab

1 carrot, peeled and chopped

1 white onion, peeled and chopped

2 celery sticks, chopped

1 garlic bulb, halved through the circumference

4 sprigs of thyme

2 star anise

2 lemons

Generous 1 tablespoon (25g) salt

Mayonnaise, as needed

Small bunch of parsley, chopped

½ cup (25g) fresh breadcrumbs

1 teaspoon Dijon mustard

4 anchovies

2 olives

1 egg, hard boiled and cooled

1. Before you cook your crab, put it in your freezer for about 45 minutes. This will slow down the crab's metabolic rate so it falls asleep.

2. Once the crab is sleeping, take a pot large enough to fit the crab and fill it three-quarters with water. Don't add the crab yet.

3. Pop the chopped carrot, onion, celery and garlic into the pot with the thyme and the star anise. Squeeze the juice from one of the lemons into the water, then add the salt. The mix should taste salty.

4. Bring this mixture to the boil and cook for 30 minutes.

5. Your mix will have developed lots of flavor by now. Top up with water if necessary and bring back up to a rolling boil. Now add the crab. Cook for 5 to 6 minutes per 1lb (450g).

6. Once cooked, turn off the heat and allow the crab to cool in the water, then discard the veg and water when you are ready to prepare the crab.

7. Your crab is made up of two different types of meat – white and brown meat. The white meat is mostly found in the two front claws and legs; you will also find some white meat in the central inner body. The brown meat is in the main body of the shell on the outer edges. Lay the crab on its back and twist off the front claws. Your next job is to remove the legs; these should easily be pulled off, then set aside.

8. Next, you need to remove the inner part of the body. I find the easiest

recipe continues on the next page

way to do this is to place the top of the crab shell onto your board upside-down, with the eyes facing away from you. Take hold of the crab with both hands and, with your two thumbs, push the inner body away from the outer shell. On the inner body you will see grey feathery gills called dead men's fingers. It is crucial to pull these off and discard, as they are inedible.

9. Using a heavy knife, cut the inner body into four. This exposes the white meat. It is a bit of a fiddle to remove the white meat from this part, but it is worth it.

10. You now need to remove the brown meat from the main shell. This can be very different crab to crab; sometimes it's firm and plentiful, other times it's not. Get what you can and put it in a separate bowl.

11. Pull off the knuckles from the claws and pick out the meat with a skewer.

12. Place the large claws on a worktop and cover with a clean towel. Smash down with the back of a heavy knife until the shell cracks. Peel off the cracked shell to extract the meat inside. There is a thin, sharp piece of cartilage in the claw – this needs removed and discarded. Do the same with both claws and the legs.

13. To check that there is no shell left in the white crab meat, place your crab meat onto a clean chopping board and with the flat of a chopping knife run it over the meat a little at a time and you will instantly feel any shell that might have been missed.

14. Using a teaspoon, scrape out the brown meat inside the main body shell, both soft and hard.

Place in a sieve and rub through into a bowl using the back of a wooden spoon.

15. You now have extracted the white and the brown meat. It is very simple to dress the crab. Your first task is to clean up the main shell. You will find that it has a band of shell that has a seam which needs to be removed; you can break off this bit along the seam. I use a clean cloth, with my thumb and forefinger.

16. Next you will need to clean the shell inside and out.

17. Take your bowl of white meat and add enough mayonnaise so that it binds the meat together. Add most of your shredded parsley, the zest from half a lemon and a squeeze of juice. Add the juice a little at a time: you want the crab to still taste of crab.

18. Now onto your brown meat. Add enough fresh breadcrumbs to the brown meat so that you get a paste type of consistency. Next add a spoonful of mayonnaise, your mustard and a little squeeze of lemon juice.

19. You are now ready to fill the shell. Taking your white meat mix first, put it in the shell at either end and leave a space in the middle for the brown mix. Fill the gap with the brown mix.

20. To finish, I have gone traditional for the plating shown opposite and used chopped anchovies, olives, the rest of the parsley and boiled eggs. The egg white and yolk have both been finely chopped and then pushed through a sieve separately.

FEATHER FOWLIE

This is a fantastic broth, and it must have one of the best names of any dish in this book. It reminds me of classical French cooking – in particular, its use of cream and egg yolks, which enrich and thicken the broth. It is a brilliant recipe and would work as an evening meal in its own right.

MAKES 10 PORTIONS

1 small chicken

2 quarts (2 liters) water, or enough to cover your chicken

2 white onions, chopped

4 sticks celery, peeled and diced

2 medium carrots, peeled and diced

4 sprigs of thyme

1 bay leaf

3½oz (100g) smoked cooked ham

2 egg yolks

½ cup (120ml) whipping cream

Small bunch of flat-leaf parsley, shredded

Pinch of nutmeg

Salt and pepper

1. Put the chicken in a pot and add the water, then bring to the boil on the stovetop. Reduce the heat and cook on a low simmer for 1 hour.

2. Next, add your vegetables, thyme and the bay leaf, and cook for a further 30 minutes.

3. By now your chicken should be cooked. Carefully remove it from the pot and set aside to cool. You might have to add more water to bring it back up to around 2 quarts (2 liters).

4. When cool enough, pick the meat from the chicken and then chop it up. Make sure you remove all tendons and gristle. You might end up with loads of chicken, so you don't have to use it all. Chop up the ham, and pop it and the chopped chicken back into the pot with the vegetables.

5. Bring to the boil, reduce the heat and allow to simmer.

6. Meanwhile whisk your egg yolks and cream together. Turn the heat off under the pot, add the cream and egg mix into the broth and fold through. The residual heat will cook the egg yolks and thicken the broth.

7. Serve scattered with the shredded parsley, a little pinch of nutmeg over the top, and seasoned with salt and pepper to taste.

CARROT & CUMIN SOUP

This is a brilliant winter warmer. The Scots have had a real love of spice for hundreds of years – the choice of spices we have today is not that much different to what was available back then. If you look through old Scottish cookbooks, spice plays a huge role in our culinary past.

MAKES 4 PORTIONS

1 tablespoon (15ml) good oil

Scant 2 tablespoons (25g) butter

1lb (450g) carrots, peeled and chopped

2 onions, peeled and chopped

2 celery sticks, washed and roughly chopped

1 leek, white only, washed and roughly chopped

4 garlic cloves, crushed

3 teaspoons ground cumin

2 tablespoons (20g) all-purpose flour

1½ quarts (1½ liters) vegetable stock (a quality cube works for this)

Salt and pepper

1. Heat the oil and butter in a deep pan over a medium heat.

2. Add all of the vegetables except the garlic and sweat gently for 5 to 10 minutes without changing color.

3. Add the garlic and cumin and cook for a minute.

4. Add the flour to absorb any excess fat and to help thicken the soup.

5. Now add the stock, bring to the boil, then turn down to a gentle simmer.

6. Cook until the vegetables are tender, then blend until very smooth; for a super-smooth soup pass through a fine sieve.

7. Season with salt and pepper to taste and serve.

GLUTEN-FREE
To adapt this recipe to make it gluten-free, change the wheat flour to gluten-free flour or just exclude flour from the recipe.

VEGAN
To make this recipe vegan, change the butter to a non-dairy alternative.

SCOTCH BROTH

Scotch broth is a hearty concoction. Historically, this type of broth would have been a staple in Scotland and northern Europe for many people, as it is a one-pot wonder. It's likely this would have been made with whatever was available at the time – so the meat, vegetables and cereals that might change season to season – but the ethos of the dish would have been the same. I have visions of this amazing broth being cooked over an open fire all day, with families coming back after a hard day's work and tucking in.

With this recipe, I wanted to make a broth that would stand up as a main meal just as it would have been. You can speed up the process or make it veggie by omitting the meat and using a stock cube. Making it traditionally takes a bit of planning, but the result is worth it.

MAKES 4 PORTIONS

2½ quarts (2½ liters) water

1lb (450g) neck of lamb or mutton (see Note)

1 medium onion, diced

3½oz (100g) carrot, diced

3½oz (100g) turnip, diced

3 celery sticks, finely diced

3½oz (100g) potato, diced

½ leek, finely diced

Scant 2 tablespoons (25ml) vegetable oil

2 cups (200g) store-bought Scotch Broth mix, rinsed and soaked overnight in the fridge (see Note)

Bunch kale, shredded

Chives, finely chopped

Salt and pepper

> To make your Scotch broth vegan, change the neck of lamb for good quality vegetable stock.
>
> Scotch Broth mix may be found at some British stores in North America, or you can substitute with 1/2 cup (100g) lentils plus 1/2 cup (100g) barley).

1. Put the water and the lamb neck into a large saucepan and bring to a simmer.

2. Skim any impurities as they rise to the surface and cook until the meat is tender. This should take about 2½ hours, depending on the lamb. Top up with a little water, if necessary.

3. Strain the stock and chill. Once it is cold, you should be able to pick the set fat off the top and discard. Cool the neck before picking and shredding the meat.

4. Add all the vegetables, except the kale, to a large pan with the vegetable oil and slowly cook over low heat for 5 minutes until they become glossy.

5. Next, add the soaked broth mix and lamb stock. Simmer until the barley and the peas in the broth mix are tender.

6. Next, add the shredded lamb neck. Cook for 5 more minutes.

7. To finish, add your shredded kale and cook until the kale is wilted.

8. Before you serve, check the seasoning and finish with a few generous turns of black pepper. Garnish with the chives.

SMOKED MACKEREL

WITH BEETS & RADISH SALAD

This is a super simple little salad and I feel it really shows off the mackerel. Smoked mackerel is jam-packed with flavor, so combining it with only a few ingredients allows it to be a real star. This is the sort of dish you can pull together for a quick lunch with whatever you have in the fridge. Smoked mackerel is traditionally hot smoked over oak chips; you can also find peppered mackerel that would work well for this recipe.

MAKES 4 PORTIONS

1 lemon
Generous ⅓ cup (85ml) good oil
1 package cooked beets
4 Brussels sprouts
4 fillets smoked mackerel
6 radishes, thinly sliced
Handful of mixed leaves
Salt and black pepper

1. Your first task is to make a lemon dressing: juice and zest your lemon and mix with the oil.

2. Cut your beets into eighths – you normally get four beets balls in each package, so you should have loads.

3. For the sprouts, remove the outer leaves and discard. Next, peel off some of the inner leaves and set aside.

4. Take your mackerel and peel off the skin, going from tail to head. Cut the fillets into 4 or 5 pieces.

5. To assemble, put a handful of mixed leaves into a bowl with the sliced radish and the sprout leaves, dress with the lemon dressing and toss the salad. Season with salt and black pepper. Add the mackerel pieces to the mix, then divide between your serving bowls. Add the beets and serve.

ARBROATH SMOKIE, CHEDDAR & BABY SPINACH PIE

Arbroath smokies are very versatile and can be used in loads of different recipes. This one is fantastic with loads of flavor. The way smokies are smoked allows that incredible but delicate flavor to transform any dish they go into.

MAKES 4 PORTIONS

For the pastry

1⅓ cups (200g) all-purpose flour
Scant ½ cup (100g) butter
1oz (25g) Cheddar cheese, finely grated
Pinch of salt
1 large egg

For the filling

1 handful baby spinach
1 Arbroath smokie
4 eggs, beaten
Scant ¾ cup (200ml) whipping cream
Scant ¾ cup (200ml) whole milk
Zest of 1 lemon
½ bunch of chives
1 small handful thyme tips
2oz (50g) smoked Cheddar, grated
Salt and black pepper

If you can't find Arbroath smokie for this recipe, smoked salmon would be a great replacement.

1. Preheat the oven to 400°F (200°C).

2. Begin by making the pastry. Rub together the flour and butter. Add the grated Cheddar and salt. Next, add the egg and bring it together carefully with your hands without overworking it.

3. Chill in the refrigerator.

4. Once your pastry has chilled, roll it out to fit an 11in (28cm) round tart pan with a removable bottom.

5. Line with parchment paper (or three sheets of plastic wrap) and baking beans, then chill again.

6. Bake blind once chilled for 10 minutes, until the pastry shell is crisp.

7. Now start making the filling. Take your spinach and give it a good wash, making sure that you have removed any grit and soil. Dry off and shred.

8. With your smokie, carefully remove the flesh and flake it, checking you have removed any of the bones.

9. Lower the oven temperature to 350°F (180°C).

10. Mix your eggs with the cream, milk, lemon zest, chives and thyme. Season with salt and black pepper.

11. Next arrange the flakes of smokie evenly into the bottom of your pastry case and top with some shredded spinach and grated Cheddar.

12. Next pour your egg and cream mix on top. I actually do this in the oven to ensure the pie is as full as possible.

13. Bake in the oven for 30 minutes or until the mix is set. Allow to come to room temperature before cutting.

BRADAN ROST

Bradan rost, or hot smoked salmon – the true translation of it simply means 'roast salmon'. This is a brilliant thing to do at home, and it is also surprisingly easy, even if you don't have your own smoker (though it is easy to make your own smoker from what is in your kitchen: I use an old tray, a cooling rack and some aluminum foil for a lid).

This method turns salmon into the most luxurious and delicious food ever. It can be used in hundreds of different ways, from mid-week pasta dishes to dinner party canapés. I make it a lot at home and have discovered that if I do it in the garden my wife doesn't give me trouble for making the whole house smell like a bonfire. The same method works with lots of different fish, from sea trout to mackerel.

MAKES 4 PORTIONS

3 tablespoons (25g) sea salt

2 tablespoons (25g) light-brown sugar or white sugar

1½lbs (675g) salmon fillet

3 tablespoons smoking chips or shavings

1. Your first job is to cure the fish. To do this, lay some plastic wrap onto a tray. Mix the salt and the sugar together, then sprinkle about half of the mixture onto the plastic wrap. Place your salmon on top of the mix and evenly sprinkle the remaining mix on top of the fish. Pull up the sides of the plastic wrap to create a parcel, then refrigerate for 3 to 4 hours.

2. While the fish is curing, prepare the smoker. First, you need to soak half of your smoking chips or shavings in water for about 20 minutes, drain and then mix with the dry chips. Put the sawdust or shavings in the base of your tray or stovetop smoker (you can line the tray with foil – it makes for easier cleaning, as you can just throw the foil away) and place a wire rack on top.

3. Once the fish is cured, rinse it under running water, then pat dry. Arrange it on the rack.

4. Cover the tray with a double layer of foil.

5. Set your tray over a medium heat. As soon as wisps of smoke start to appear, or you can smell the smoke, reduce the heat to low and smoke the fillets for about 20 minutes.

6. Turn the heat off and wait until you can't see any more smoky wisps, then open the smoker and check that the fish is cooked through. It should be opaque and not at all glassy-looking. If it isn't quite cooked through, you can put the heat on again or you can finish the fish in the oven.

7. You can eat this straight away or wrap it in plastic wrap and, once cool, refrigerate for up to 2 days. If you want to serve it later and have it hot, you can reheat it, wrapped in foil, in the oven on a medium heat.

HAM HOCK
& RED LENTIL SOUP

As far as I know, red lentils are not grown in Scotland, or even in the UK for that matter, but red lentil soup has become a Scottish staple. I think it fits our weather. When you incorporate some ham hock into it, I can't think of anything more homely or Scottish.

During the winter months, I always have soup in the fridge. More often than not it is this very recipe. It is a real crowd pleaser and a family favorite; it is also a simple thing to make. You can skip the ham hock stage and replace it with vegetable stock to speed up the process.

MAKES 4 PORTIONS

1 ham hock (you will get all the stock you need from this)

1 tablespoon (15ml) good oil, plus extra for garnish

1 onion, peeled and chopped

2 celery sticks, peeled and chopped

2 carrots, peeled and chopped

1 garlic clove, crushed

1¼ cups (250g) split red lentils, thoroughly washed

4 teaspoons tomato paste

1 bay leaf

Bunch of green onions, shredded, for garnish (optional)

Salt and black pepper

1. The first job is to sort out the ham hock. In days gone by, the ham hock would have needed to be soaked overnight; these days, I find the ham not overly salty, so it can be cooked on the same day. Place the ham into a large pot and fill it with water, then bring it to the boil.

2. Once boiled, remove the ham from the pot and discard the water. Giving the ham a blanch will get rid of most of the impurities and will help you obtain a better base stock. Put the ham back in the same pot and top up with more water.

3. Cook, simmering for 2½ to 3 hours, until the ham starts to fall off the bone.

4. Once your ham is cooked, remove from the pot, pick the meat off the bone, shred and set aside. Strain your stock and set aside. You are going to need 2 quarts (2 liters) minimum.

5. Heat the oil in a pan. Add the chopped onion and cook over a low heat for 5 to 6 minutes, until beginning to soften.

6. Stir in the celery and carrot and cook for 2 minutes. Add the garlic and cook for a further minute.

7. Add the washed lentils and 2 quarts (2 liters) of your ham stock, the tomato paste and a bay leaf.

8. Bring to the boil, reduce the heat, cover the pan with a lid and simmer for 20 to 25 minutes until the lentils and vegetables are very soft.

9. Remove the bay leaf from the soup and discard. Next, add the shredded ham hock.

10. Check the consistency. It will be fairly thick, so if you prefer it thinner, add a little more stock. Season with salt and pepper to taste. Serve, topped with a drizzle of oil and some shredded green onions.

LANGOUSTINE COCKTAIL

This is a classic. At one point it would have been the height of sophistication to serve a prawn cocktail at a dinner party. It hit our tables in the early seventies and has never really left. I have a recipe on the menu at my restaurant, Creel Caught, very close to this one and it's brilliant to see it going out, especially to our younger guests who might be having one for the first time. I have upgraded this with some stunning Scottish langoustine.

A point to note: if you allow your frozen North Atlantic prawns to defrost in the bag overnight in the fridge, the flavor is so much better.

MAKES 4 TO 6 PORTIONS

16 fresh Scottish langoustine
9oz (250g) North Atlantic prawns
1 avocado, halved and diced
½ iceberg lettuce, shredded
1 baby gem lettuce, shredded
4 green onions, finely chopped
12 cherry tomatoes, halved
¼ cucumber, chopped
4 radishes, sliced
½ lemon

For the dressing

7 tablespoons (100ml) white wine
    vinegar
2 tablespoons Dijon mustard
1 tablespoon wholegrain mustard
1 teaspoon superfine sugar
Juice of ½ lemon
Salt and pepper
Scant ¾ cup (200ml) good oil

For the cocktail sauce

⅓ cup (100g) mayonnaise
1½ tablespoons tomato ketchup
1½ tablespoons sweet chilli sauce
Dash of Worcestershire sauce
1 teaspoon paprika, plus more for
    garnish
Squeeze of lemon juice
Dash of brandy
Salt and pepper
Dill, chopped, for garnish

1. To start, you need to get the langoustine prepared. Boil a pan of lightly salted water and add the langoustine. Cook for roughly 3 minutes – time will depend on their size.

2. Remove from the water and place on a plate or board to cool – do not run under water, as this will waterlog the meat and means it will lose flavor. Once cool, peel, making sure that the waste tract is removed and discard.

3. To make the dressing, pop all the ingredients (minus the oil) in a bowl and whisk until dissolved. Slowly drizzle the oil in, whisking constantly until you create an emulsion.

4. For the cocktail sauce, put all the ingredients into a bowl and mix. Adjust the seasoning to taste.

5. Mix the North Atlantic prawns in the cocktail sauce. Squeezing the prawns gently will help remove any excess moisture.

6. Toss the salad vegetables together and dress with the dressing.

7. The most important part of making a prawn cocktail is to build it properly, so it is vital that you construct it in such a way that every mouthful has a good mix of ingredients. I always start by putting prawns in the glass first and, with this one, I would put a langoustine in each glass too. Then layer some dressed salad on top and then some more prawns.

8. Tower the cooked langoustine on top with a dollop or tablespoon of the cocktail sauce. Garnish with paprika and dill. Serve with brown bread and butter.

PARTAN BREE

This is another wonderful soup from the north-east of Scotland. Partan is old Scots for crab and bree is old Scots for soup or broth. This is one dish that really reminds me of my days starting out as a chef. For me at that time, this type of luxurious flavor was alien, but I soon fell in love with fish and shellfish through making and enjoying this dish. I also managed to include this in an episode of *MasterChef: The Professionals*.

You can use a pre-cooked crab for this, but you most definitely need the shells. This recipe and method will also work with lobster and langoustine, giving a subtler and sweeter flavor.

MAKES 4 PORTIONS

1 whole live brown crab (or whatever crab is local to you)

2 tablespoons (30ml) good oil

Scant 2 tablespoons (25ml) brandy

1 white onion, chopped

3 cloves garlic, chopped

2 sticks celery, chopped

2 carrots, chopped

6 tomatoes, chopped

½ cup (100g) basmati or long grain rice

1 teaspoon paprika

1 bay leaf

Salt and pepper

½ lemon

1 cup (250ml) white wine

¼ cup (50g) tomato paste

Scant ¼ cup (50ml) whipping cream

Few knobs butter

1. Your first task is to cook your crab. There are many different schools of thought on how best to kill the crab. I suggest putting it in the freezer for around 30 minutes. This will slow down its metabolism to such a low level that it will peacefully go to sleep and when it's cooked it will be completely unconscious.

2. Bring a large pot of water to the boil. Make sure your pot gives the crab plenty of room and bear in mind the water displacement. Once your crab is asleep, add it to the water but only once it's come to a rolling boil. (If you are using brown crab, I recommend boiling it in heavily salted water for about 12 minutes per 2lb (900g)).

3. Once cooked, remove the crab from the water and allow it to cool. Do not immerse it in ice water – I find the crab becomes waterlogged and it can affect the flavor.

4. Now you can remove the meat from the crab. The brown meat is really rich, tasty and creamy. The white meat is delicate and sweet.

5. Pull off the two large claws and crack them open with the back of a heavy knife. Carefully pick out the meat, which is known as white meat, making sure you pick out any small splinters of shell.

6. Turn the crab shell upside down and remove the legs. Next, hold the crab with both hands, with the rounded part of the shell on the table, and, using your thumbs, push the body away from the top shell to expose the inside of the crab. This is where you'll find the brown meat. This varies in color and texture but is all edible.

7. Ensure the gills or 'dead man's fingers' are removed – these are grey and feathery and are not edible.

8. There is also some white meat in the shoulders of the small legs, which can be picked out with the help of a metal skewer.

9. You are now ready to make the soup. In a large saucepan cook the crab shells in a little oil for 5 mins. Add a splash of brandy.

10. Add the chopped onion, garlic, celery and carrot, and fry for a further 5 mins. Add the chopped tomatoes, rice, paprika, bay leaf and season with salt and pepper. Stir well.

11. Add a squeeze of lemon juice, the white wine, tomato paste and 1 quart (1 liter) of water.

12. Bring to the boil and then gently simmer for 1 hour, skimming the surface periodically to remove scum.

13. Add the brown meat to the soup and cook for a further 10 minutes.

14. Pass through a fine-meshed sieve, return to the saucepan and gently reduce to half the volume. Gently whisk in the whipping cream and butter until the sauce thickens. Next, fold in your white crab meat, double check your seasoning and serve.

SMOKED HAM HOCK TERRINE

I have been making this recipe for years. I love the fact that you end up with the most delicate and tasty dish ever. I have included a smoked ham hock in this recipe, as I think it adds something really special to the dish.

This makes one terrine – using a 4½in (11cm) x 12in (30cm) x 4in (10cm) terrine mold – but you can set it in anything you wish, for example in a tray and cut into flat rectangles.

MAKES 1 TERRINE

2 unsmoked ham hocks

1 smoked ham hock

2 sprigs rosemary

2 sprigs thyme

1 bay leaf

4x 4½in (11cm) sheets gelatin

Small bunch chives, chopped

2 green onions, sliced

Small bunch flat-leaf parsley, shredded

3 tablespoons (50g) Arran mustard (you can use any wholegrain mustard)

2 tablespoons (25g) capers, halved

About 3 gherkins, chopped

1. Place the ham hocks, rosemary, thyme and the bay leaf into a large pan and cover with cold water. Bring to the boil.

2. Reduce the heat and let it gently simmer until the meat starts to fall off the bone. Throughout the cooking, make sure you skim off the froth. This should take about 3 to 4 hours.

3. When ready, strain the cooking liquid into a separate pan and set aside.

4. Remove all the meat and gelatinous fat from the bone. Pop your gelatin into a bowl of ice water to soften up. This is called blooming. Blooming gelatin is important, as it really helps the gelatin to fully melt in whatever you are using it for.

5. Shred the meat, making sure you remove any fat or sinew. Set aside in a large bowl.

6. Take 1⅔ cups (425ml) of your cooking liquid and heat in a pot on the stovetop. Just before it comes to the boil, remove from the heat and add your softened gelatin. Mix well. This will be your stock.

7. To the bowl with the meat, add the stock, and the chives, green onions, shredded parsley, Arran mustard, capers and gherkins.

8. Give it a good mix and transfer into your terrine mold. It is up to you what you set it in – traditionally it would be set in a cast-iron terrine mold, but you can choose.

9. This is brilliant served with any kind of fruit or onion chutney (recipes on page 36 to page 39), and some homemade oatcakes (recipe on page 221) on the side.

APPLE CHUTNEY

This is a fantastic recipe that has so many uses. If done properly, it can be kept for months in sterile jars. The ginger adds another little dimension; when it comes to which apples to use, I tend to opt for an apple that tastes great and holds up to the long cooking, as most of it will break down but some of it will keep a bit of texture.

MAKES 3 TO 4 JARS

1lb (450g) white onions

2lbs (900g) Braeburn apples

1 cup (150g) raisins

1in (3cm) fresh ginger, grated

1 teaspoon ground ginger

4 garlic cloves, crushed

2 teaspoons mixed spice

2½ cups (500g) light brown sugar

2 cups (500ml) cider vinegar

1 small bunch of thyme

2 sprigs of rosemary

Generous 1 tablespoon (25g) salt

½ teaspoon black pepper

1. Your first job is to wash, peel and rewash your onions, then chop them.

2. Next wash and peel your apples, quarter and core them, and then cut each piece into 6.

3. Place the onions, apples, and all the other ingredients into a large pan. Slowly bring to the boil, stirring the whole time, then lower the heat so that the chutney cooks at a rolling boil. Stir the chutney regularly, making sure it does not catch and burn, until it is thick and sticky. A good way to check if it is cooked is to draw your wooden spoon across the chutney – if the spoon fills up with runny liquid, the chutney is not ready yet.

4. Remove any thyme and rosemary stalks.

5. Once cooled, you can store the chutney in sterile jars.

RED ONION CHUTNEY

I always have some red onion chutney to hand in the fridge. It has made a huge resurgence in recent years, and for good reason: red onion chutney is so versatile and works well with some strong mature cheese as well as on a burger. We have loads of brilliant producers in Scotland who make onion chutney but giving it a go is very rewarding.

MAKES 3 TO 4 JARS

6 medium red onions

1 tablespoon (15ml) good oil

2 garlic cloves, finely chopped

1 red chilli, finely chopped

⅓ cup (50g) raisins

1 bay leaf

1 teaspoon coriander seeds

½ stick cinnamon, broken up

¼ cup (50g) light brown sugar

7 tablespoons (100ml) red wine vinegar

7 tablespoons (100ml) port

Pinch of salt

1. Peel and halve the onions through the root. Then slice the onion with the grain; you are trying to avoid the rainbow cut as the onion breaks down too much doing this.

2. Heat the oil in a large pan on a low heat, add the onions, garlic, chilli, raisins and bay leaf, and cook gently for 20 minutes, stirring occasionally.

3. Make a spice bag using a small square of cheesecloth and a piece of string. Wrap up all the spices, tie up tight and add to the pan.

4. Once the onions are cooked and translucent, add the sugar, vinegar and port and stir well. Simmer on a low heat for 30 to 40 minutes, stirring occasionally until the chutney is thick, dark and sticky.

5. Remove and discard the spice bag.

6. Once cooled, you can store it in sterilized jars.

GLEN COE

COMFORT FOOD

CHICKEN BALMORAL

CABBAGE, BACON & CREAMY GRATIN POTATOES

This dish is a huge hit in my house. When we ask visitors what they would like for dinner, they always ask for the same dish – and it's this one. It is super simple and packed with flavor. With the crisp skin of the chicken, and the spice and texture of the haggis, what's not to love?

The first thing you will need to have organized is the creamy gratin potatoes. The good news is this can be done in advance. If you don't have time, or are looking for something a bit healthier, this dish works well done simply with boiled new potatoes.

MAKES 4 PORTIONS

1 savoy cabbage

4 chicken breasts, skin on

10oz (300g) haggis (you can always make your own – see recipe, page 65)

6 rashers dry cured bacon

3 tablespoons (50g) wholegrain mustard

1 small bunch chives

1. To prepare the cabbage, remove the outer leaves and discard; these leaves are normally very dark and sometimes damaged. Cut the root off and start to remove the leaves; you will be able to remove most of the leaves until you get to the center. Remove and discard the center spine of each leaf.

2. Shred the leaves by rolling them up tightly and running your knife through the leaves as thinly as you can until all the leaves have been cut. With the center core, quarter it and shred; there is no need to remove the center spine as it is very tender.

3. Preheat the oven to 400°F (200°C).

4. Blanch the cabbage in rapidly boiling water, then drain in a colander and cool with ice cold water.

5. You now need to prepare your stuffed chicken breasts. You do this by placing the chicken breast skin side down on the chopping board, then carefully make an incision from top to tail of the breast, without going all the way through. Open up the incision on each side to make a pocket.

6. Take about 3oz (85g) of haggis and roll it into a long sausage shape the same size as the cut in the chicken. Place the haggis into the space in the chicken then cover and roll. Repeat for each chicken breast.

recipe continues on the next page

7. In a hot pan, sear your chicken breasts, skin side down first, until crisp and golden. Remove from the pan, place onto a roasting tray and pop into the oven for about 15 minutes or until the thickest part of the chicken reaches 167°F (75°C).

8. While the chicken is in the oven, finish preparing the cabbage. Take your bacon and cut it into thin strips, pan fry until cooked, then add the blanched cabbage, chopped chives and wholegrain mustard and mix well.

9. Once your chicken breast is cooked you are ready to serve.

Creamy Gratin Potatoes

1¼ cups (300ml) whipping cream
Scant ¼ cup (50g) butter
3 garlic cloves, crushed
1 sprig of thyme
1 sprig of rosemary
Salt and pepper
About 1½lbs (675g) potatoes, peeled and thinly sliced
3½oz (100g) smoked Cheddar cheese, grated

1. Preheat the oven to 350°F (180°C).

2. In a thick-bottomed pot, add the cream, butter, garlic, thyme and rosemary, and bring to a boil.

3. Season with salt and pepper.

4. Once the cream has boiled, strain, return to the pot, add the sliced potatoes, and slowly simmer until the cream starts to thicken. This is the starch coming out of the potato. It also helps speed up the cooking process in the oven, as the potatoes have started cooking.

5. Next, carefully layer the potatoes into a baking tray. I like to add a little grated cheese between each layer as I go.

6. Scatter the top layer with cheese, cover your tray with aluminum foil and place into the oven.

7. Bake for 20 minutes, remove the aluminum foil and bake for a further 15 to 20 minutes or until a knife can easily be inserted into the potato.

BEEF OLIVES

This is a dish I grew up with. I distinctly remember loving beef olives in the school lunch hall. I always use what I know as beef ham for them; I had to phone a butcher friend of mine whilst writing this to find out what cut of beef provides beef ham. Traditionally beef olives would have been wrapped in pig's caul fat to hold them together, but I think a cocktail stick is much more user-friendly.

MAKES 4 PORTIONS

For the beef olives

3½oz (100g) smoked bacon, diced

1 medium onion, chopped

3 garlic cloves, peeled and crushed

4 sprigs of thyme

12oz (350g) sausage meat

1 cup (50g) fresh breadcrumbs

8 thin slices of top round

Salt and black pepper

For the sauce

2 medium onions, chopped

4 carrots, peeled and sliced

4 garlic cloves, peeled and crushed

¼ cup (50g) tomato paste

1¼ cup (300ml) beef stock, a carton or quality cube would work for this.

⅓ cup (50g) all-purpose flour

7 tablespoons (100ml) red wine

For the beef olives

1. In a pan, add a little oil, and your diced bacon, and gently cook. Next, add your chopped onion and soften without coloring.

2. Add your garlic and thyme, and cook for a couple of minutes.

3. Once cooked, take off the heat, remove any thyme stalks and set aside to cool.

4. Put your sausage meat into a bowl. Once the onion and bacon mixture is cooled, add to your sausage meat, along with your fresh breadcrumbs and a few twists of black pepper and some salt.

5. Give this a good mix and divide into 8 balls, which you then roll into sausage shapes.

6. Lay your slices of top round onto your work surface and place a sausage of stuffing on each slice of meat, roll up to make your olive and secure each of them with a cocktail stick.

7. Preheat your oven to 300°F (150°C).

For the sauce

1. Now move on to your sauce. In a pan, add a little oil, then add your chopped onion, cook until they have become translucent, and add your carrots and garlic.

2. Next add the tomato paste and cook for a couple of minutes, add a little splash of stock and then add your flour. Give it a good mix. You are aiming for a paste type of consistency.

3. Now add about half of your wine and cook until reduced by half.

4. Once it has come to the boil and all of your tomato paste and flour have been dispersed, you can add the remaining wine and the stock and bring back to the boil.

To assemble

1. Pop your beef olives into a casserole dish and cover with the sauce. Cover the dish and pop into the oven for 1½ hours or until the top round has cooked.

2. Allow to cool – and remember to remove the cocktail sticks!

SHEPHERD'S PIE

Shepherd's pie has loads of regional variations around the UK. This is how I make it for my family; it is a complete meal for us, and it is one of those dishes that I place onto the middle of the table and everyone helps themselves. Some sources suggest that the shepherd's pie originated in Scotland, but in a slightly different form, as it was topped with pastry, hence the name 'pie'. It wasn't until the recipe reached the shores of Ireland that it got its potato topping.

MAKES 4 PORTIONS

1 tablespoon (15ml) good oil

1lb (450g) ground lamb

1 onion, finely chopped

3 carrots, chopped into ⅓in (1cm) dice

5oz (150g) chestnut mushrooms, sliced

2 garlic cloves, crushed

2 tablespoons tomato paste

1x 14oz (398ml) can chopped tomatoes

Scant ¾ cup (200ml) beef or lamb stock (a good quality cube will work for this)

3 tablespoons (45ml) Worcestershire sauce

1lb (450g) potatoes, cut into chunks (see note on p.50)

1 tablespoon (15g) butter

Salt and pepper

1oz (25g) white Cheddar, grated

1. Heat the oil in a large, deep pan over a medium heat.

2. Once the pan is hot, add in the ground lamb. (You can test the heat by putting in a little bit of meat and if it makes a sizzling noise it's hot enough.) Don't tip all the meat in; place enough into the bottom of the pan so that it covers the base and separate it. If you have to do this stage a couple of times, it will be worth it. Don't shake or shoogle the pan; allow the ground lamb to brown. Lots of caramelization at this stage will create loads of flavor. Once all the ground lamb has been browned, remove from the pan and set aside.

3. Next, add the onion and carrots. Fry for about 8 minutes until they start to soften. Add the mushrooms and garlic, then fry for a further 5 minutes. It's important that the crushed garlic enters the pan at a cooler stage in the process, as it reduces the risk of burning.

4. Add the ground lamb and stir to combine, then cook for 3 to 4 minutes.

5. Add the tomato paste, chopped tomatoes, stock and Worcestershire sauce, then simmer for 25 minutes.

6. Heat the oven to 400°F (200°C).

7. Meanwhile, put the potatoes in a pan of water and bring to the boil. Cook until tender.

8. Drain in a colander and allow to 'steam out'; this gets a good bit of the water out of the potatoes, as all the steam that you see is moisture that you don't need. Return the potatoes to a dry pan and put back onto a medium heat. This stage achieves two things: it gets the potatoes back to being nice and hot (having the potatoes piping hot is vital when mashing them); it also helps to get rid of more moisture.

9. After a couple of minutes you are ready to mash with the butter, salt and pepper.

10. When the ground lamb mixture is cooked, pour into a 1½ quarts (1½ liters) ovenproof dish, then spoon or pipe the mash on top to cover.

11. Sprinkle with the cheese. Bake for 30 minutes until melted and golden, and the sauce is bubbling around the edges.

12. Leave it to stand for 5 minutes, then serve.

MINCE & TATTIES

This is a dish I make often at home – it's so simple and all the kids love it. I remember when I was growing up that mince and tatties was a dish we had loads back then; the mince and onions were just boiled in water and then thickened with gravy granules. My method involves browning the onions and the ground beef – this will give you loads of flavor and depth. I also like to add lots of carrots into the mix, but this is optional. Most families have their own recipe, so feel free to add whichever vegetables you like.

MAKES 4 PORTIONS

For the mince

2 medium onions, finely diced

1½lbs (675g) lean ground beef

⅓ cup (50g) flour, optional

9oz (250g) carrots, peeled and diced

Salt and pepper

Splash Worcestershire sauce

For the tatties

1lb (450g) potatoes (see below)

Scant 2 tablespoons (25g) butter

Scant 2 tablespoons (25ml) whole milk

Salt

The secret to great mashed potatoes is to follow some very simple rules. Make sure you use the correct potato (Maris Piper, King Edwards, or Desiree). Peel the potatoes with a potato peeler and not a knife, as you will save putting loads of potato in the bin. And don't cut the potatoes up too small, as they tend to break up and that makes the mash watery and starchy.

1. Preheat the oven to 300°F (150°C).

2. Next, finely dice your onion, pop them into an oven-proof pot and place onto the stovetop.

3. Slowly cook the onions until they start to color. Once they are golden brown, remove them from the pot and set aside. Put the pot back on the stovetop.

4. Add a little oil to the pan and you can now start adding the ground beef. I tend to do this a little at a time, as I do not want to overload the pan. You want to make sure that you always have a good sizzle while you are browning. This process will really help develop flavor in the dish.

5. Next, dust in your flour; the flour will help thicken the overall dish.

6. Add your cooked onions and diced carrots, and enough water so that you have just covered the ground beef.

7. I always cook stuff like this in the oven – long and slow at 300°F (150°C). The reason I do this is so that I do not need to keep stirring it. So, pop a lid on your pot and place it into the oven for 1 hour.

8. Once cooked, double-check the seasoning. I like a few good turns from the pepper mill. Finish with a splash of Worcestershire sauce. (I know this is not Scottish, but it tastes amazing.)

For the tatties

1. Place the potatoes in a deep pan, cover with cold water and a pinch of salt, and bring to the boil slowly. Don't keep stabbing them with a knife, as it breaks them up.

2. Once the water comes to the boil, turn it down to a simmer and cook until tender.

3. Drain the potatoes in a colander and allow them to steam out for a few minutes. Place back into the pan and dry out slightly over a low heat.

4. Now, mash until smooth, then add butter and milk, making sure you do not allow the potatoes to cool down. I think the best way to mash them is through a potato ricer, though a mouli grater makes the job easy and provides you with lump-free mash, and saves loads of time.

5. Season to taste.

BRAISED SHOULDER OF BEEF

WITH SUET DUMPLINGS

Suet dumplings have been made for hundreds of years, not only in Scotland but in the whole of the UK and Ireland, and were especially popular during hard times. Dumplings are very inexpensive to make and great at filling you up. Cooking the dumplings in the sauce, in my opinion, is the best, as they take on loads of flavor. They are absolutely delicious when they soak up the meat juices from the beef.

MAKES 4 PORTIONS

For the beef

2 tablespoons (30ml) good oil

1¾lb (800g) shoulder of beef/chuck beef, diced

Scant 2 tablespoons (25g) butter

2 sticks celery, peeled and diced

4 shallots, peeled and diced

3½oz (100g) carrots, peeled and diced

1 clove garlic, crushed

⅓ cup (50g) flour

¼ cup (50g) tomato paste

Scant ⅔ cup (150ml) red wine

3 sprigs rosemary

Small bunch thyme

1 cup (250ml) beef stock (pre-made carton stock works for this)

Salt and pepper

For the dumplings

⅔ cup (100g) self-rising flour (see note on p. 201)

2oz (50g) beef suet

Pinch of salt

Small bunch chives, chopped

¼ cup (60ml) cold water

For the beef

1. Preheat your oven to 275°F (140°C).

2. In a large pan suitable for the oven, heat the oil.

3. Season the beef and once the pan is nice and hot add the meat. Brown over a high heat until evenly caramelized, then remove from the pan and set aside.

4. Add your butter to the pan and over a lower heat soften the vegetables for 3 to 4 minutes, then add the garlic.

5. Add the flour. This will absorb any excess fat and help the sauce to thicken.

6. Add the tomato paste and cook for a minute, followed by the wine, which you need to reduce by two-thirds.

7. Add the beef back to the pan, along with the herbs, then add the stock and bring it up to the boil.

8. Check seasoning and place the lid on the pan, then pop into your oven for 1½ hours.

9. Meanwhile, make the dumplings. (See the steps below this method.)

10. When ready, take the pan out of the oven and add your little dumplings.

11. Spoon over some sauce, pop the lid back on, and put back in the oven until the beef is tender and the dumplings have tripled in size, about 20 minutes.

For the dumplings

1. Sift the flour into a bowl, add the suet and mix well.

2. Add a pinch of salt and your chives.

3. Make a well in the center, add the water and mix lightly to form a smooth paste.

4. Flour your hands and roll the paste into ¾in (2cm) balls, place on a tray and add to your stew at the appropriate time.

SLOW ROAST SHOULDER OF LAMB

When I pick an ingredient to cook at home, I always think flavor first. Shoulder of lamb is delicious and jam-packed with flavor. This recipe is a slow and moist method of cooking lamb, and shoulder lends itself to this perfectly. It is a cut that is better cooled long and slow, and as a bonus you get the best gravy ever at the end.

MAKES 4 PORTIONS

1 shoulder of lamb

Salt and pepper

Splash of good oil

4 onions, peeled and thinly sliced

3 carrots, peeled and chopped

½ leek, halved, sliced and washed

6 cloves garlic, peeled and chopped

6 sprigs thyme

3 sprigs rosemary

1½ cups (350ml) white wine

1½ cups (350ml) lamb stock (a quality cube works for this)

Fresh thyme and/or mint, if desired

1. You will need a thick roasting dish that can also go on the stovetop. Preheat the oven to 400°F (200°C).

2. Lightly season the lamb with salt and pepper, and rub all over with a little oil.

3. Put the lamb into the roasting dish and cook in the oven for 25 minutes until golden.

4. Remove from the oven and turn the oven temperature down to 275°F (140°C).

5. Add the onions, carrots, leek, garlic, thyme and rosemary to the dish and mix well.

6. Cover the dish with aluminum foil and cook in the oven for 1 hour.

7. Take the dish from the oven and remove the foil.

8. Give the vegetable mixture a good stir. Add the wine and half the stock to the dish, place on a low heat on the stovetop and bring to a simmer.

9. Cover the dish, pop it back into the oven and cook for a further hour. Remove from the oven, add the remaining stock and return to the oven for a further 30 minutes.

10. The vegetables should be golden and the sauce syrupy – if not, pour the vegetables and liquid into a pot and boil until it gets to that consistency.

11. Remove the lamb from the dish, place on a large serving plate and spoon over the sauce. Serve with a spoon and a fork, as the meat will fall off the bone.

12. The lamb can be sprinkled with some freshly picked thyme leaves or freshly shredded mint.

SMOKED HADDOCK
MAC 'N' CHEESE

I have always considered mac 'n' cheese to be a Scottish dish. I know it's pasta, but growing up and watching my mum make it from a tartan package, what else would I think? Marshalls pasta company has been making pasta for over a hundred years and, what's more, it's made in Glasgow. Macaroni is a staple for most families in Scotland and we are now five generations in using Glasgow's own. I have put it on menus for years, and have even sold it in Scottish restaurants I have opened and called it Scotland's very own pasta dish. Changing it up a little by adding smoked haddock really lifts it. If you are feeling indulgent, lobster is also a fantastic addition.

MAKES 4 PORTIONS

For the sauce

1 small onion

1 bay leaf, optional

2 cloves, optional

2 cups (500ml) whole milk

9oz (250g) pale smoked haddock

Scant ¼ cup (50g) butter

2oz (50g) all-purpose flour

2oz (50g) Cheddar cheese, grated

Salt and pepper

For the pasta and veg

1 teaspoon good oil

2 leeks, finely sliced

9oz (250g) macaroni

3½oz (100g) Cheddar cheese, grated

4 tablespoons white breadcrumbs

For the sauce

1. Peel your onion, then using the cloves pierce the bay leaf onto the onion. Place the studded onion into a small pot and cover with the milk. This is a classic, but I still do it.

2. Next, remove any bones that might still be in your haddock and place the fillets into the milk. This is going to do a couple of things: cook the haddock and flavor the milk. This will then flavor the whole dish.

3. Slowly bring the milk up to a simmer, then turn off the heat and allow the studded onion and the haddock to infuse.

4. Melt the butter in another small pan, then add flour and mix to form a thick paste called a roux.

5. Carefully remove the haddock and set aside.

6. Meanwhile, cook your roux for 3 to 4 minutes, then slowly start to add the warm flavored milk and then the Cheddar cheese. Stir continuously while the milk and cheese are added until you achieve a smooth sauce with the consistency of thick whipping cream. If you add the milk a little at a time, you will avoid making a lumpy sauce.

7. Simmer for 10 minutes over a very low heat to avoid burning the sauce, stirring every minute or so.

8. Once cooked, cover with plastic wrap or parchment paper to avoid it skinning.

For the pasta and veg

1. Heat the oil in a large, lidded pan over a low heat. Add the leeks, cover and cook for 5 minutes until tender.

2. Meanwhile, cook the macaroni in a large pan of boiling salted water as per the package instructions until al dente. It shouldn't be completely soft as it will continue to cook when baked. Drain and set aside.

3. Meanwhile, preheat the oven to 375°F (190°C).

4. Add the sauce to your cooked leeks with half of the cheese. Add the cooked pasta, then gently fold in the cooked smoked haddock and place into an ovenproof baking dish.

5. Top with the remaining cheese, then scatter the breadcrumbs over the top.

6. Bake in the oven for 20 to 25 minutes until golden and bubbling around the edges. Serve immediately.

STOVIES

I have been holding off writing this recipe, as I haven't been one hundred per cent sure what the definitive stovie recipe is. As it turns out, I don't think there is one: no two recipes are the same. The common denominator seems to be stock, and some sort of meat and potatoes. I have seen things like Lorne sausage going in, though more commonly it would be leftover Sunday roast beef or lamb. The differences are not even regional – it changes from family to family. My problem in developing my own recipe is I never, ever had stovies in my house growing up. So this recipe is how I would like them made today.

The word 'stovie' means 'to be cooked on a stovetop'. The nature of this dish was simply not to waste food, so you could add whatever you like and it would still be a stovie.

MAKES 4 PORTIONS

Scant 2 tablespoons (25g) butter

2 medium onion, finely chopped

½ yellow turnip, peeled, chopped into ¾in (2cm) dice

2 carrots, peeled, chopped into ¾in (2cm) dice

2 celery sticks, peeled, finely chopped

½ leek, diced

1½lbs (675g) roast lamb or beef

1¾lb (800g) potatoes, peeled, diced

2 cups (500ml) beef or lamb stock, a quality cube works for this

¼ savoy cabbage, shredded

Salt and black pepper

1. Heat the butter in a large pan. Add the chopped onion and cook on a low heat for 10 minutes until softened.

2. Add the turnip, carrot, celery and leek, and cook for 5 minutes.

3. Dice and stir in the cooked meat, then add the potatoes.

4. Pour over the stock and season generously, bring to the boil, then turn the heat down to a simmer.

5. Cover and cook for 1½ hours or until the vegetables have softened and the potatoes have broken down completely.

6. Once the vegetables are cooked, you can stir in the shredded cabbage. Cook for a further 10 to 15 minutes until the cabbage is bright green.

7. Stovies are traditionally served with oatcakes, but I prefer crusty sourdough bread.

THE QUIRAING, ISLE OF SKYE

HAGGIS

Haggis, neeps and tatties, p.66

HOMEMADE HAGGIS

This has got to be – by a country mile – the most well-known Scottish dish. It even has the grand title of being Scotland's national dish. It has been the butt of jokes the world over: some people think it was invented as some sort of dare, while others think it's a creature that has one leg shorter than the other and spends most of its time running round the hills.

One of Robert Burns' most famous works is all about this humble creation and it takes center stage on the 25th of January every year at thousands of Burns Night suppers the world over.

Haggis has been made in Scotland since ancient times. The fact of the matter is that many countries have very similar dishes, using up the offal of sheep and lambs, but it's the Scottish haggis that has stood the test of time. The word 'haggis' first appeared in print, believe it or not, in an English cookbook by the writer and poet Gervase Markham in 1615. Haggis, and dishes similar to it, were developed out of necessity, as nothing went to waste on an animal.

But before I continue I have a confession: I had never made haggis in my life up until a couple of years ago when I was a presenter of a BBC Scotland show called *Landward*. My segment on the show was following the journey of some of my favorite foods and the people who make them. I was very keen to explore the Isle of Mull, as it's a place I totally love and is the ancestral home of the Macleans. I have a friend who lives on Mull, Flora Corbett, and she is a real foodie, so I enlisted her help in finding me the very best of what the island had to offer.

She instantly suggested we film a show with the haggis lady of Mull, Jeanette Cutlack. Perfect, I thought, this couldn't get any better. In my mind, the haggis lady of Mull was a wise elder in the community who could share her knowledge of haggis with me. She owned a croft in Ballygown, her closest neighbour living six miles away, and she'd turned her home into a small restaurant, with her speciality, of course, being haggis. Not just any haggis – one of the only haggises made in the Hebrides.

The day of filming arrived and the crew and I made our way to the west coast of the island. When we arrived at the croft, I knocked on the door and was met by a young English woman; this was the famous haggis lady of Mull! Jeanette had moved to Mull from the south of England a few years earlier to experience island life. I found the story got better . . . She had made haggis for the first time to support her son's school's Burns Night supper and it was so good she was asked by everyone to make more – a legend was born.

This is not Jeanette's recipe but is as close to the method as I remember.

1 sheep's or lamb's stomach (you can buy artificial casing online)

1 lamb's or sheep's pluck (liver, lungs and the heart, see note below)

2 cups (200g) rolled oats

1 cup (100g) steel-cut oats

3 white onions, chopped

Scant 2 tablespoons (25g) butter

4 teaspoons allspice

1 teaspoon salt

7oz (200g) suet

4 teaspoons ground black pepper

Finding a sheep's pluck may be difficult in North America as I think sheep lungs are not available to buy. My advice would be use the same amount of liver and heart and substitute the lungs with 1lb (450g) of minced pork or chicken (rather than adding more liver, for example, which would increase the offal flavor too much). Add the minced pork or chicken at step 9 of the recipe.

1. Your first task is to sort your lamb's stomach: wash and then place in a bowl of salted water, then pop in the fridge overnight. Your butcher will be able to help with the casing, or you can buy an artificial one online.

2. Your next job is to prepare the pluck. Rinse it in cold running water. Place it into a large pot, cover with cold water and bring it to the boil. Reduce the heat and simmer for 2 hours.

3. Meanwhile, toast your rolled oats and oatmeal in the oven for 10 minutes.

4. In a separate pan slowly cook and soften your chopped onions with the butter.

5. Once your oats have cooled, mix with the allspice, salt, pepper and suet.

6. Remove the pluck from the cooking liquid, but make sure you keep the cooking liquid as you will need it later.

7. Cut the cooked heart, liver and lungs up into smaller pieces, making sure you remove and discard the windpipe, fat and gristle.

8. Pop all of the cooked meat into a food processor with the onions and blitz down. Be careful not to break it down too much, as you want to keep some of the texture.

9. Mix this with the suet and oats. Now add some of the cooking liquid to the mix. You are looking to make the mix a little runny – a kind of lava-type consistency.

10. Tie one end of your stomach closed, then carefully add your mix to the open end. You will get in a bit of a mess at this stage.

11. Next bunch the stomach up until you get a ball of haggis. Starting at the bottom, tie some string around it to make smaller haggis balls; as you tie each bung, make sure you try and get out as much air as possible – don't fill it too much either, as this mix will expand during cooking.

12. Next you need to cook the haggis. The best way to do so is to boil them in the same cooking liquid that you used for the pluck. So, strain the cooking liquid and top it up with more water if necessary.

13. Add your haggis, bring to the boil, then reduce the heat and simmer for 3 hours.

14. Once cooked, carefully drain the cooking liquid and allow the haggis to sit for 10 minutes. You can then eat straight away or reheat at a later date.

HAGGIS, NEEPS & TATTIES

WITH SKIRLIE

This is the classic and probably the most traditional way of serving haggis; it's just a bit of a fiddle to shape and keep hot. Lots of chefs simply stack it into a ring and heat up all three elements in the oven, then remove the ring. I had a chance meeting at my restaurant with Hilda McBain, who is known to her family as the Skirlie Girly because her skirlie is so good – so naturally I had to have her recipe in the book. She uses Cookeen vegetable fat for her recipe, but if you struggle to find that, just use butter. Skirlie is a very traditional Scottish dish made from oatmeal, shallots, fat, and seasoning. It makes a great stuffing or a topping and is delicious stirred through mashed potatoes or sprinkled on top of a dish. It adds loads of flavor and texture and in tougher times would fill hungry bellies.

The secret to making great mashed potatoes is to use the right kind – Maris Piper, King Edwards or Desiree work best. Do not cut the potatoes too small or they tend to break up and mash watery and starchy. For that same reason, don't stab them too much with a knife or fork.

MAKES 4 PORTIONS

For the neeps

1 medium yellow turnip or
    rutabaga, diced
2 carrots, diced
Scant ¼ cup (50g) butter
Salt and pepper

For the skirlie

Scant ¼ cup (50g) butter
2 shallots, diced
2 sprigs rosemary
2 sprigs thyme
1 cup (100g) rolled oats

For the neeps

1. Cook the turnips and carrots in a pan of boiling water for 20 to 25 minutes until very tender.

2. Drain well and leave to steam-dry in the colander for 10 minutes. Return the vegetables to the pan along with the butter, then mash using a potato masher. Mash it how you like it – having a little texture works well. Season with lots of black pepper.

For the skirlie

1. Melt the butter in a pan. Add the diced shallots and herbs, and cook until the shallots are translucent.

2. Add the oats and stir until all the butter has been absorbed, then season with salt and pepper.

3. Cook for a further 5 minutes, stirring all the time. Be careful it doesn't burn, keep the mixture moving!

For the tatties

1lb (450g) potatoes (Maris Piper, King Edwards or Desiree), peeled and diced

Salt

Scant ¼ cup (50g) butter

Scant ¼ cup (50ml) whole milk

The heating of the haggis

You will need about 1lb (450g) for 4 people (you can always make your own – see recipe, page 65)

For the tatties

1. Place the potatoes in a deep pan. Cover with cold water, add a good pinch of salt and bring to the boil slowly.

2. Once the water comes to the boil, turn down to a simmer and cook until tender.

3. Drain the potatoes in a colander and allow to steam out for a few minutes, then place back into the pan and dry out slightly over a low heat.

4. Now mash until smooth, then add butter and milk, making sure you do not allow the potatoes to cool down. I think the best way to mash them is through a potato ricer, or a mouli grater makes the job easy and provides you with lump-free mash and saves loads of time. Taste for seasoning.

The heating of the haggis

There are a number of ways to heat up your haggis; it all depends on how you buy it. If you are buying the small bungs in natural skins, heat according to the instructions. If it's a log or a can, you have two options: pop the haggis into a microwave bowl, add a little water and heat until piping hot. Alternatively, you could put it in a saucepan and heat it on the stovetop.

Or you could make the haggis yourself! Go to page 65 for my homemade haggis recipe.

HAGGIS DICED GARLIC POTATOES & POACHED EGG

This can easily be made vegetarian by using veggie haggis, which is remarkably close to real Scottish haggis. The good news is that it is also widely available in most supermarkets; in the USA it is sold as veggie crumble. This is also super quick to make; the main skill needed here is poaching an egg. Once you understand how to make them, they are so easy to do and can be prepared in advance.

MAKES 4 PORTIONS

¼ cup (60ml) white vinegar

4 eggs

1lb (450g) frying potatoes, diced (Maris Piper work brilliantly)

1lb (450g) package of haggis (you can always make your own – see recipe, page 65)

2 cloves garlic, crushed

Bunch flat-leaf parsley, shredded (optional)

1. Poach the eggs first. I know what you are thinking – you would have probably done them last. But you can poach eggs in advance using this method.

2. Take a medium pan of water and add a generous amount of vinegar, taste the water and if you don't make a funny face you need to add more vinegar; it should be acidic. (One small note to this is don't add any salt to the water – the salt affects the egg white and breaks it down.)

3. Carefully crack your eggs into four separate little cups or ramekins. To start cooking the eggs, take your little cup with the egg inside and slowly submerge the cup into the water. Once the cup is full of the hot water, carefully release the egg from the cup. By doing this, the egg is not dropped in the water, therefore the yolk is surrounded in the white. Add all your eggs the same way. One other thing to note: the water doesn't need to boil.

4. After a few minutes, the eggs should be ready to remove from the water with a slotted spoon. Take them out one at a time and submerge into ice-cold water to stop the cooking process. This also washes away the vinegar.

5. Now your eggs are ready, preheat the oven to 400°F (200°C).

6. Heat oil in a frying pan. Add the potatoes and fry until golden and crisp.

7. Crumble in the haggis and cook until it starts to crisp up too, then add the crushed garlic and cook for a couple of minutes.

8. Meanwhile reheat your poached eggs in some simmering salted water.

9. Add the shredded flat-leaf parsley to the haggis and potato mix, if you are using it.

10. Split this mixture into four dishes and top with your beautiful runny poached egg.

HAGGIS & SWEET POTATO SAUSAGE ROLLS

Haggis sausage rolls are a great way to use haggis as a party snack. I've added lots of ingredients, including sweet potato, which works well with it and gives it a bit of color and a different texture.

MAKES 4 PORTIONS

1 tablespoon (15ml) vegetable oil

2 shallots, chopped

3½oz (100g) sweet potato, peeled and diced

7oz (200g) pork sausage meat (you can use a couple of sausages for this)

7oz (200g) haggis (you can always make your own – see recipe, page 65)

12oz (350g) frozen puff pastry

1 egg yolk, beaten

1. In a small pan, heat a little oil, then add the shallots and the sweet potato and cook slowly. Once the shallots have become translucent and the sweet potato is almost soft, remove from the heat.

2. Meanwhile, remove the sausage meat from their skins and pop into a bowl with the haggis. Once the shallot mix has cooled, add to the bowl also. Mix well.

3. You are on to the fun part now. Remove the pastry from the packaging and carefully roll it out. When doing so, be very gentle. Keep turning it to ensure you roll it nice and evenly. You can get away with rolling it very thinly for sausage rolls, as you don't need as much puff.

4. Cut three sections of pastry about 4in (10cm) long each from the roll.

5. Lay out the pastry, weigh out roughly 5oz (150g) of your sausage mix, and shape into a long cylinder and place lengthwise at the closest edge of the pastry.

6. Brush the exposed part of the pastry with a little of the egg yolk.

7. Next, turn the pastry over the sausage meat, making sure you create a tight roll. Repeat for the other sheets of pastry.

8. Pop your sausage rolls onto a lightly floured or oiled tray and put in the fridge for 10 minutes until they are nice and firm. At this stage preheat your oven to 400°F (200°C).

9. Remove your tray from the fridge, brush your sausage rolls with more egg yolk, and using a sharp knife score the top of the pastry.

10. Bake in the oven for 20 to 25 minutes until golden brown.

11. Allow to cool and cut to your preferred size.

HAGGIS SCOTCH EGGS

This is a brilliant alternative to a traditional Scotch egg. Incidentally, a Scotch egg is not of Scottish origin – the humble food has a murky and confusing past, with claims to its invention coming from Fortnum & Mason and the British Army, and even possibly a butcher in Yorkshire. Some say it has a connection to Indian cuisine! But one thing's for sure – it is not Scottish.

In order for this to be classified as a Scottish delight, I have added one of our most famous foods: haggis. As you will discover going through the book, haggis is very versatile and it works really well in loads of recipes. The reason for this is the seasoning of haggis is perfect for enhancing anything that you might add it to. It also adds texture and moisture.

MAKES 4 PORTIONS

4 medium eggs

6oz (180g) haggis (you can always make your own – see recipe, page 65)

6oz (180g) sausage meat

Small bunch chives, chopped

Generous ⅓ cup (60g) all-purpose flour, seasoned with salt and pepper

7 tablespoons (100ml) whole milk

1 egg, beaten

2 cups (100g) fresh breadcrumbs

2 cups (500ml) vegetable oil, for deep-frying

1. Your first task is to boil the eggs. There is much debate on how to do this. Some say boil from cold water and then set a timer; others say add the eggs to boiling water. I have been experimenting and think that if you start with cold water they are much easier to peel. So take a pan, place your eggs in it and top it up with cold water. Bring the water to the boil. Set your timer for 5½ to 6 minutes as soon as the water comes to the boil. Once cooked, cool immediately.

2. Peel and set aside. We need very soft-boiled eggs so that they are still runny when we break open our finished Scotch egg.

3. Next, place your haggis, sausage meat and chopped chives into a bowl and mix together. This is probably best done by hand. You should end up with a sticky mix. This shouldn't need any seasoning at all, as the haggis does this for you.

4. Divide the mixture into four even balls.

5. Take a sheet of plastic wrap and place onto your surface. Pop one of the balls onto the plastic wrap, then place another sheet of plastic wrap over the top and flatten using circular movements with your hands. You should end up with a nice, even flat circle of mix.

6. Remove the top layer of plastic wrap, place one of your soft-boiled eggs on top of the mix and, using the bottom layer of plastic wrap, pull the mix around the egg – keeping the bottom layer of film in place will help you shape the mix without getting all messy and sticky. Keep your egg wrapped in the film and repeat for the other three eggs.

7. The next thing you need to do is breadcrumb the eggs. To do this you will need what's called a pané system. This consists of three trays: one with seasoned flour, one with the milk and egg mixed together and one with the breadcrumbs.

8. Unwrap your eggs one a time and drop into the flour first, then the egg and milk mix, and lastly the breadcrumbs.

9. Preheat your oven to 350°F (180°C).

10. Heat the oil in a heavy-bottomed pan until it reaches 350°F (180°C). Deep-fry the Scotch eggs for 2 minutes, or until golden.

11. Carefully remove the eggs and drain on paper towel.

12. Pop on a baking tray and bake for 8 to 10 minutes, or until the sausage meat and haggis are cooked through. You can serve them straight from the oven, or eat them the next day from the fridge.

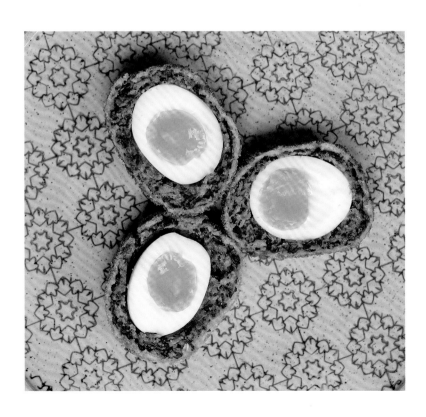

HAGGIS PITHIVIER

This is another brilliant way of using haggis. These little pies are incredible! They work well as a little snack or equally as an appetizer with some whisky sauce.

MAKES 4 PORTIONS

10oz (300g) haggis/veggie haggis (you can always make your own – see recipe, page 65)

5oz (150g) pre-rolled puff pastry

1 egg and a splash of whole milk, for egg wash

1. Preheat the oven to 350°F (180°C).

2. Break up the haggis in a food processor, then mold it into small balls, about ¾in (2cm) in size.

3. Cut discs measuring 2½in (6cm) from the sheet of pastry, remembering you need 2 discs per pithivier.

4. Brush one disc from each portion with egg wash, then place the haggis ball in the center.

5. Put the puff pastry top on and press the discs together tightly around the haggis, expelling as much air as possible. Re-cut the pastry so the pithivier is nice and neat.

6. Brush with egg wash and bake for 10 to 12 minutes until piping hot.

HAGGIS BON BONS

WITH WHISKY MUSTARD SAUCE

Haggis bon bons are a relatively new invention, having become popular over the last twenty years or so. But you will rarely attend a fancy event and not get offered these as a canapé. For this recipe, I have used breadcrumbs, but they work well with steel-cut oatmeal as well.

I always try to serve haggis in the different countries I work in. I have served these to more than 200 chefs at events in India, and I have also presented them at the British Consulate in Havana, Cuba. Predictably, everyone loves them. They are a great introduction to haggis.

MAKES 4 PORTIONS

For the bon bons

1lb (450g) haggis (you can always make your own – see recipe, page 65)

2 eggs

A splash of whole milk

All-purpose flour, for rolling the haggis

3½oz (100g) Panko breadcrumbs

For the whisky mustard sauce

1 white onion

Good oil

1 carrot, finely diced

Scant ¼ cup (50ml) whisky

7 tablespoons (100ml) red wine

1 teaspoon all-purpose flour

1¼ cup (300ml) brown chicken stock or vegetable stock

3 sprigs thyme

7 tablespoons (100ml) whipping cream

3 tablespoons (30g) Arran mustard or wholegrain mustard

Pinch chives, chopped

For the bon bons

1. Break the haggis up in a food processor, then remold it into about 20 small balls.

2. Mix together the eggs and the splash of milk and set out on a plate. Lay out separate plates with the flour and breadcrumbs.

3. Roll the haggis bon bons first in the flour, then into your mix of egg and milk, and finally into the breadcrumbs.

4. Place in the fridge for a few hours to set.

5. Deep fry at 340°F to 350°F (170°C to 180°C) for 3 to 4 minutes until piping hot in the center.

Whisky mustard sauce

1. Wash, peel and rewash your onions, then slice them as thin as you can. Cut with the grain (follow the lines on the onion) and avoid cutting rainbow shapes as they are all different sizes and will break up too much when cooking.

2. Add the onions with a little oil to a wide-bottomed pan and place on the stovetop on low heat. Caramelizing the onions is a long and slow process; you want to color the onion without high heat as this gives the best flavor.

3. Once the onions have achieved a golden brown color, add the finely diced carrots.

4. Add the whisky, followed by the red wine. Bring to the boil and boil until the wine is reduced by half. Sprinkle the flour in, add the brown stock and thyme, and reduce till the sauce thickens.

5. Pass the sauce through a sieve into a clean pot, then add the cream, chopped chives and mustard.

6. To serve, pour a little of your sauce into some shot glasses and top with your crispy haggis bon bons.

HAGGIS KOFTAS

WITH YOGURT & MINT

This recipe helps add seasoning and moisture to the dish; I always use haggis in every kofta that I make. These are great cooked on the barbeque or simply in the oven.

MAKES 4 PORTIONS

2 onions

6 garlic cloves, crushed

1 small bunch of flat-leaf parsley, shredded

1lb (450g) ground lamb

1lb (450g) haggis (you can always make your own – see recipe, page 65)

2 teaspoons dried chilli flakes

1 teaspoon ground cumin

1 egg

Salt and freshly ground black pepper

⅔ cup (200g) Greek yogurt

½ cucumber, diced

1 small bunch of mint, shredded

Oil for brushing

8 bamboo skewers, soaked in water overnight (this stops them burning)

1. Your first task is to grate your onions, then add to a bowl with the garlic and parsley.

2. Mix in the ground lamb and the haggis.

3. Next, add the chilli flakes, ground cumin, egg, 1 teaspoon of salt and some freshly ground black pepper.

4. Mix together with your hands until the mixture has bound together.

5. Preheat your oven or broiler to 400°F (200°C).

6. Divide the mixture into 8 and then mold each piece into a long sausage shape around a drained bamboo skewer. I used a sausage maker for this, but you don't have to.

7. Brush the kofta generously with oil and place onto a tray.

8. Cook for 10 minutes, turning them now and then, until browned all over and cooked through.

9. Meanwhile, mix the yogurt with the shredded mint, diced cucumber and a pinch of ground cumin.

10. Serve the koftas with the mint yogurt. Enjoy!

HAGGIS PAKORA

WITH ARRAN MUSTARD & WHISKY RAITA

This is a fantastic way of using up leftover haggis. It has become a very famous dish in its own right – and a bit of a Scottish legend.

MAKES 4 PORTIONS

For the pakora

7oz (200g) haggis (you can always make your own – see recipe, page 65)

1 red onion, finely diced

½ package baby spinach, shredded

½ bunch cilantro leaves, shredded

1 green chilli, finely diced

1 teaspoon chilli powder

1 teaspoon ground cumin

½ teaspoon ground coriander

1 teaspoon tandoori masala powder

Salt and pepper

Scant ¾ cup (200ml) cold water

3⅓ cup (300g) chickpea flour

Oil for deep frying

Sliced red onion and a pinch of garam masala, for garnish

For the raita

1¼ cup (300ml) natural yogurt

½ bunch mint, picked and shredded

1 teaspoon Arran mustard, wholegrain also works

1½ tablespoons (25g) tomato ketchup

2 teaspoons (10ml) whisky

½ teaspoon garam masala

For the pakora

1. Place the haggis, vegetables and herbs into a large bowl.

2. Add all the spices, salt and pepper.

3. Add the cold water and with your hands, start mixing the water, vegetables and spices.

5. Now gradually add in the chickpea flour. Fundamentally, you are trying to achieve a consistency that is sticky and moist. It is not like a batter; it is much more like a paste. Add more chickpea flour, if needed.

6. To cook the pakora, in a large pot, heat the oil to about 330°F (165°C) – this is a much slower style of deep-frying, as you need to cook out the vegetables and the flour. (I always do a little test batch to make sure I have the seasoning correct, and adjust it as needed before frying the rest.)

7. To begin preparing the pakora, you will need a little bowl of water nearby. Dip your hands in the water and, with wet hands, take a golf-ball-size amount of mix and flatten it out, then carefully place it into the hot oil. Fry until crispy. Repeat until all the mixture has been used up, working in batches as needed.

8. When ready to serve, top with a little sliced red onion and a dusting of garam masala.

For the raita

1. Place the yogurt in a bowl.

2. Add the shredded mint leaves, mustard, ketchup and whisky. Whisk.

3. Check the seasoning and finish with a dusting of garam masala.

HAGGIS SLIDERS

These are a great party food and should attract people who wouldn't usually eat haggis. Normally, when you make burgers there is a certain amount of skill and practice in getting the seasoning correct. The great thing about adding haggis to the mix is that the seasoning is done for you, giving the burger an amazing flavor. It also helps to hold in the moisture.

MAKES 12 SLIDERS

1lb (450g) haggis (you can always make your own – see recipe, page 65)

1lb (450g) ground beef

Salt

Good oil

12 slider buns, toasted

2 plum tomatoes, sliced

2 red onion, sliced

2 large dill pickles, sliced

Your favorite relish

Lettuce leaves

12 small slices smoked Cheddar cheese

1. To make the burger, it's as simple as mixing the haggis and the ground beef together and adding a little salt.

2. In my opinion, burgers should be pressed. A butcher would have a fancy pressing machine; at home you can recreate this by using a plastic lid. Find one that's about 2½in x ¾in (6cm x 2cm), then place the lid on the work surface and cover it with plastic wrap. Take some of your mixture and press it into the plastic wrap-covered lid. Get as much of the mixture in as you can, then fold over the plastic wrap, upturn the lid and push down onto the work surface. Remove the lid and plastic wrap.

3. To cook the burger, heat up a griddle pan or frying pan on high heat, add a little oil, then place the burger into the pan. The secret is not to touch the burger or turn it over until it has a chance to brown. With the burgers being so small, they will cook very quickly, about 5 to 10 minutes in total.

4. Once cooked, build your burgers using the buns, tomatoes, red onion, pickles, relish, lettuce and cheese. I like as many layers as possible. This will make every mouthful different.

LOCH CRAIGNISH, NEAR CRINAN

FISH & SHELLFISH

ARBROATH SMOKIE

The Arbroath smokie is a spectacular Scottish delicacy, and one of very few foods in Scotland that has Protected Geographical Indication (PGI) status. This gives the smokie protection from impersonators; Arbroath smokies can only be made within 5 miles of Arbroath! This recipe does not tell you how to make a smokie at home but rather how to heat one up; you can prepare the smokie in advance, keep it in the fridge and then heat it up when you're ready.

Every year I am a guest chef at the Dundee Flower and Food show. I always look forward to this event, not just because it is fantastic, but because come lunchtime I can get a smokie straight off the barrel. Eating a smokie like that is in my top ten food experiences.

When I was first developing the menus for my seafood restaurant, the first dish I wanted on the menu was a smokie; I wanted to do my best to recreate that experience in Edinburgh that I got every year in Dundee. So I spent a lot of time testing ways to heat it up and I came up with this method.

MAKES 4 PORTIONS

Generous ⅓ cup (85g) butter, room temperature

Small bunch dill, roughly chopped

Salt and pepper

½ lemon

4 Arbroath smokies

1. First make your dill and lemon butter: add the soft butter to a small bowl, add your chopped dill, a few twists of pepper, a pinch of salt and a squeeze of lemon juice, and give it a good mix. Place this in the fridge to set.

2. Cut four squares of parchment paper – about the same length of the smokie – and set aside.

3. Cut four squares of aluminum foil, bigger than the square of parchment.

4. Chop your dill butter up into cubes.

5. Lay your four squares of aluminum foil onto the table, and the four sheets of parchment paper on top of the aluminum foil.

6. Next place a smokie on top of the parchment, then a couple of cubes of the dill butter into each smokie.

7. Next pull up the edges of the aluminum foil, and create a loose bag from the foil making sure you crimp the edges so that the fish is sealed in a aluminum foil bag.

8. When you are ready to heat up, preheat your oven to 350°F (180°C) and place your aluminum foil bags onto a tray and place them into the oven. The cooking time could be between 10 and 15 minutes depending on how big the fish is.

9. I would serve them in the bag and let your guest open it – the room will fill with the wonderful smokie aroma.

HERRINGS IN OATMEAL

Herring is considered a delicacy in Europe, but in Scotland we hardly ever use it. It's a pity, because it's a fantastic fish full of flavor, and it's healthy. Similar to sardines, herring is abundant in the North Sea, especially off the coasts of Shetland.

This recipe is really simple, and it's the first one I think of when I want to have herring. I am a fan of letting the professionals do what they do best – that's why I always suggest that you let your fishmonger do the hard work of filleting fish. And although it's not traditional, for this recipe I coat the fish with breadcrumbs; the egg also creates a seal and helps keep in the moisture.

MAKES 4 PORTIONS

4 herrings, filleted and pin bones removed

Generous ⅓ cup (60g) flour, seasoned with salt and pepper

1 egg

Splash whole milk

1 cup (100g) rolled oats

4 tablespoons (60ml) good oil

Scant 2 tablespoons (25g) butter

1 lemon

Salt and pepper

1. To coat the fish with breadcrumbs, you will need what's called a pané system. This consists of a tray with seasoned flour, one with an egg and a little milk, and a third tray with the oatmeal.

2. Drop your fillets into the flour first, then the egg and milk mix, and lastly the oatmeal.

3. You are now ready to cook your fish. Heat the oil in a large frying pan and fry the fish over medium heat for 4 minutes each side.

4. Reduce the temperature and add your butter. Baste the fish in the butter until golden.

5. Finish with a squeeze of lemon and then serve.

HOT SMOKED SALMON SALAD NIÇOISE

I think that hot smoked salmon actually works better than the traditional tuna Niçoise. The flavor from the smoked salmon is incredible. Warming up the salmon first really changes the eating experience and lifts the smokey flavor all through the dish. Store-bought hot smoked salmon is easy to find but it is worth giving it a go yourself. There is a brilliant recipe on page 27.

MAKES 4 PORTIONS

Generous ⅓ cup (85ml) good oil

Scant 2 tablespoons (25ml) white wine vinegar

½ teaspoon Dijon mustard

10oz (300g) hot smoked salmon

12 new potatoes, cooked and sliced

1oz (25g) green beans, blanched

16 cherry tomatoes, halved

12 olives, pitted, cut into halves

4 eggs, soft boiled, 6 minutes

Handful of arugula

Handful of Swiss chard

Salt and pepper

1. First, prepare a simple dressing by combining your oil, vinegar and mustard.

2. Preheat your oven to 325°F (160°C).

3. Place your hot smoked salmon onto a baking tray and put it into the oven to warm through for 5 to 7 minutes.

4. Next, heat a non-stick pan, add a splash of oil, then add the potatoes. Sauté for 4 to 5 minutes until they are golden in color.

5. Add the beans and cook for 1 minute, then toss in the tomatoes and olives and warm through for a further minute. Place this mixture into a bowl and spoon over half of the dressing.

6. Take the salmon out of the oven and flake it into the potato mix. Cut the egg in half or quarters and place around the potato mix. Dress the arugula and Swiss chard with the remaining vinaigrette and add to the center of the bowl.

7. Season to taste.

MI-CUIT SALMON

WITH BEET CHUTNEY,
BABY GEM LETTUCE & APPLE SALAD

This is a nice way to cook salmon. When I say cook, the direct translation of mi-cuit is 'partially cooked'. In a professional kitchen, this would be done sous vide in a water bath, but I have found at home it can easily be done in the oven.

MAKES 4 PORTIONS

For the mi-cuit salmon

4x 5oz (150g) salmon fillets, skin on

¼ cup (50g) sugar

⅓ cup (100g) salt

1 quart (1 liter) cold water

2 teaspoons (10ml) good oil

For the beets chutney

9oz (250g) cooked beets, diced

1 Braeburn apple, grated

2 medium white onions, diced

1 cup plus 2 tablespoons (125g) light brown sugar

Generous ⅓ cup (85ml) red wine vinegar

Zest and juice ¼ orange

¼ teaspoon ground ginger

¼ teaspoon coriander seeds

¼ teaspoon mustard seeds

¼ cinnamon stick

Pinch ground cumin

Pinch cayenne powder

recipe continues on the next page

For the mi-cuit salmon

1. The first job is to brine the salmon. To do so, mix the sugar, salt and water until everything is dissolved. Place the salmon in a deep dish and cover with the brine. Soak for 30 minutes in the fridge.

2. Remove the salmon from the brine and pat dry. Pop into a small oven dish and cover with the oil.

3. Place the dish into your oven set at 100°F (37°C) for 1 hour. If your oven doesn't go that low, set it at the lowest temperature it can go to.

4. Remove from the oven and cool, and once cold place in the fridge until set.

5. Lastly, make the crispy skin; this is a very simple thing to make. Remove the scales from the salmon and scrape all the flesh from the inside of the skin. Season with salt and place between two trays. Bake in the oven at 325°F (160°C) until crisp.

For the beets chutney

1. This is a super simple recipe. All you have to do is prepare all the ingredients and then place them into a suitable-sized pan on the stovetop, bring up to the boil, then turn down to a gentle simmer.

2. Cook the chutney slowly for about 45 minutes to 1 hour, or until the majority of the liquid has gone. You should be left with a sticky chutney.

For the Caesar dressing

⅔ cup (150g) mayonnaise

6 anchovy fillets, canned or brined

1oz (25g) parmesan, grated

1 tablespoon (15g) Dijon mustard

½ lemon

Salt and pepper

For the apple salad

2 green apples

½ lemon

⅓ cup (85g) mayonnaise

Salt and pepper

½ baby gem lettuce

For the Caesar dressing

1. With a hand blender, blitz all the ingredients except the lemon.

2. Adjust seasoning with lemon juice, salt and pepper.

For the apple salad

1. Peel and dice the apples, then squeeze a little lemon juice over the apples.

2. Mix with the mayonnaise and season with salt and pepper.

3. Wash and tear the baby gem lettuce.

4. Combine all the ingredients to make the apple salad.

To serve

1. Carefully place the ingredients onto each serving plate, finishing with the dressing.

SCALLOP & BLACK PUDDING

WITH POTATO & GREEN APPLE

As a chef and educator, I love the fact that I don't just teach the practical elements of cooking but also highlight and share knowledge of wonderful ingredients and sustainability.

This is a relatively simple dish, but it relies on great ingredients and precise cooking to make it stand out. Two of Scotland's most iconic ingredients marry beautifully to make this classic dish. I always use hand-dived scallops because it is the most sustainable method of harvesting this incredible ingredient. Black pudding is a real speciality of Scotland; Stornoway black pudding is particularly good. Black pudding has been made in crofts on the Hebridean Isles for hundreds of years. It is so unique that in 2013 it was awarded Protected Geographical Indication (PGI) status.

You can get scallops in the shell from most good fishmongers. They will be more than happy to shuck them for you. If you fancy giving it a go yourself, it is very easy. You will need a table knife and a spoon for the job. You will notice that the scallop has a rounded and a flat shell. Insert your knife into the hinge of the shell and twist to pop open. Run your knife along the inside of the flat shell to separate it from the meat. Once you have the shell completely open, take your spoon and scoop everything out. You now need to remove the white meat and the roe from the skirt; I do this by separating them with my fingers. Discard all excess material so you are left with white juicy meat and roe. Give them a quick clean under cold water, and your scallops are ready to cook and enjoy!

1lb (450g) potatoes, diced (good frying potatoes work best)

Good oil

1lb (450g) black pudding, diced

3 cloves garlic, crushed

4 king scallops in the shell, shucked

Scant 2 tablespoons (25g) butter

½ lemon

Small bunch flat-leaf parsley, shredded

1 green apple, cut into matchsticks

1. Preheat your oven to 400°F (200°C).

2. Next, place some oil and the diced potato into your frying pan. Fry until golden and crisp, about 5 to 10 minutes. You want to make sure that the potatoes have started to go soft, then add the black pudding.

3. Cook until the pudding starts to crisp up, then add the crushed garlic and cook for a couple of minutes.

4. Pop all of this onto a baking tray and place in the oven until the potatoes are cooked.

5. Meanwhile, give your pan a clean, pop it back on the stovetop on high heat and, once hot, add a little oil.

6. Next, place each scallop into the pan. Try not to shake or shoogle the pan – you want to create lots of color on the scallop before turning it.

7. Once you have colored both sides of the scallop, reduce the heat and add your butter and a squeeze of lemon juice.

8. Baste the scallop in the butter and lemon. Once cooked, remove from the pan.

9. Now take the potatoes and the black pudding out of the oven, mix in the shredded parsley and double-check the seasoning.

10. Fill each of the cleaned shells with the potato and black pudding mixture. Top each one with a scallop and finish with your apple matchsticks.

SEARED FILLET OF SALMON

WITH A POTATO & GREEN ONION SALAD, CAPERS & BROWN BUTTER

This is a quick and easy dish, using baby new potatoes to make a light and tasty salad.

Learning how to make brown butter is a great skill to pick up. Browning changes the whole dynamics of butter; it goes from something that is rich and creamy to sharp and nutty.

MAKES 4 PORTIONS

10oz (300g) new potatoes

4 green onions, finely shredded

Bunch dill, chopped

½ cucumber, finely diced

7 tablespoons (100ml) crème fraîche

Good oil

4x 4oz (125g) salmon fillets

Butter

Salt and pepper

1 lemon

¼ cup (40g) capers

1. Pop the potatoes in a pan, cover with water, add a pinch of salt and bring to the boil. Once boiling, turn down and simmer until tender. Be careful not to overcook. Drain and allow to cool naturally in the colander.

2. Slice the potatoes and place in a bowl. Add the shredded green onions, dill and cucumber.

3. Bind this together with the crème fraîche.

4. In a pre-heated non-stick frying pan, add a teaspoon of oil, then add the salmon and color well on both sides – about 2 to 3 minutes for each side - working in batches if necessary. Add a knob of butter to the pan and baste. Season with salt and pepper.

5. Remove the fillets from the pan and cook the butter until its starts to brown. Remove from the heat, squeeze in half a lemon and add the capers.

6. Place your potato salad onto serving plates, add the salmon, top with the butter and capers, and a drizzle of oil if you like. Serve with a wedge of lemon.

STEAMED MUSSELS

I believe that Shetland mussels are some of the best in the world. The flavor is unbelievable. This recipe forms the bestselling dish in my restaurant, Creel Caught. We use over 660lbs (300kg) of mussels per week.

Mussels are one of the most sustainable farmed foods in the world because of how they grow. Their aquaculture is zero-input, meaning that they don't need food or fertilizer; rope-grown mussels like Shetland mussels can provide a habitat for other creatures, and they also clean the water. I was lucky enough to go on a mussel harvest in Shetland and I have been addicted to them ever since.

MAKES 4 PORTIONS

4½lbs (2kg) fresh mussels
2 shallots, finely diced
¼ leek, diced and washed
Scant ¼ cup (50g) butter
Salt and pepper
Scant ¾ cup (200ml) white wine
½ bunch flat-leaf parsley, chopped
Squeeze of lemon, plus lemon wedges to serve

1. The first job is to clean the mussels. Wash them under cold running water and, using a table knife, scrape away any barnacles. You also have to remove the beards that protrude from between the closed shells. (If you manage to source Shetland mussels, the cleaning should be easy, as they come in very clean and have very few barnacles.)

2. If you find any mussels are open, give them a short little tap on the side of the sink. This should encourage them to close. If they don't close, they should be thrown away.

3. Place the cleaned mussels into a bowl, then add the chopped shallots, leek, butter, salt, pepper and wine.

4. For this dish, you will need a large pot with a tight-fitting lid. My method for preparing mussels is to cook them very, very quickly. To do this, place the pot onto the heat and make it as hot as you can without burning it.

5. Pour in the mussels with the rest of the ingredients and, quick as you can, place on the lid.

6. The idea is that the heat from the pot creates instant steam, cooking the mussels very quickly.

7. Resist the urge to look in the pot, as you will lose the steam and stop the cooking. Another thing to avoid is shaking the pot. If you shake the pot, the mussels will simply fall out of their shells.

8. After a few minutes, if you have managed to keep the steam in, the mussels should be cooked. Have a little look, and if the mussels are wide open, they are ready.

9. Spoon the mussels into your serving bowls, discarding any that have not opened.

10. To finish, sprinkle with chopped parsley and a squeeze of lemon juice. Serve with a couple of lemon wedges.

SMOKED HADDOCK KEDGEREE

Kedgeree is one of those dishes that has been claimed by the Scots. It first appeared in a Scottish cookbook in the 18th century. I learned that it was devised by a Scottish regiment whose troops had returned from India and were looking for a little taste of something to remind them of their time there. It's the combination of smoked haddock and spice. What's not to like?

MAKES 4 PORTIONS

3 cups (750ml) vegetable stock (a good quality stock cube would work for this)

1lb (450g) un-dyed smoked haddock

Scant 2 tablespoons (25ml) vegetable oil

2 banana shallots, finely chopped

1 teaspoon ground coriander

1 teaspoon ground turmeric

2 teaspoons curry powder

9oz (250g) basmati rice

1 bay leaf

4 eggs

Small bunch flat parsley, shredded

Small bunch cilantro, shredded

Few sprigs dill, shredded

Salt and pepper, for seasoning

1. Your first job is to cook the smoked haddock. Bring your stock to the boil in a large, shallow pan and add the smoked haddock fillet. Simmer for 4 minutes, until the fish is just cooked.

2. Lift it out onto a plate and leave until cool enough to handle. Keep the stock – it will now have loads of smokey flavor. Top up with water to 1 quart (1 liter) and set aside for later.

3. In a large, lidded pan, heat the oil, add the shallots and gently fry for 5 minutes until softened but not colored. Add the spices, season with salt, then continue to fry until the mix starts to go brown and smells fragrant; about 3 minutes. Be careful at this stage not to burn the spices.

4. Add the rice and bay leaf, and stir in.

5. Add your cooking liquid from poaching the haddock, stir, then bring to the boil. Reduce to a simmer and cover for 10 minutes.

6. Take off the heat and leave to stand, covered, for 10 to 15 minutes. The rice should be perfectly cooked if you do not lift the lid before the end of the cooking.

7. Meanwhile, boil your eggs by carefully placing them into a pot of boiling water for 6 to 7 minutes (if you like your eggs hard-boiled, 8 to 10 minutes will be plenty of time).

8. Once the timer is up, make sure you cool the eggs immediately to stop the cooking process. Once cooled, peel and quarter the eggs.

9. To serve the kedgeree, fold your shredded herbs and the haddock through the rice (removing and discarding the bay leaf), and top up with the quartered boiled eggs.

SOUSED HERRING

Soused herring is a very traditional way of preserving fish. Don't be mistaken that this will be similar to supermarket rollmop herring – this dish is beautiful and uses one of our most underused fish.

Before the oil boom in the North-East, herring fishing was vital to the local economy and this style of dish would have been commonplace. This is another recipe that would have been developed out of necessity, in order to preserve the fish before the invention of the fridge.

MAKES 4 PORTIONS

4 herrings, filleted
2 teaspoons salt
Scant ¾ cup (200ml) cider vinegar
7 tablespoons (100ml) water
¾ cup (150g) sugar
2 shallots, finely sliced
1 carrot, finely sliced
6 juniper berries, crushed
2 sprigs thyme
4 fresh bay leaves
Pinch cayenne pepper
1 teaspoon peppercorns

1. First, salt the fish. This will draw out the moisture and create a firmer flesh. Lay your fillet out on a tray skin side down, sprinkle with salt, cover with plastic wrap and pop in the fridge for a couple of hours.

2. Meanwhile you can make your pickling liquid. Add the rest of the ingredients – the cider vinegar, water, sugar, sliced shallots, sliced carrots, juniper berries, bay leaves, thyme, cayenne, and the peppercorns and the sugar – to a pot and bring it to the boil.

3. Remove from the heat and let stand for 10 minutes.

4. Preheat your oven to 300°F (150°C).

5. Take the fish from the fridge and wash off the salt, then pat dry with kitchen paper.

6. Strain the pickling liquid. Put the liquid to one side, and save the bits and bobs left in the sieve (remove and discard the bay leaves). These will be used to stuff the fillets. Simply lay out the fillets, place some of the mix at the tail end and roll up.

7. Place the rolled fillets into a baking dish. You are looking for the rolled fillets to fit snuggly.

8. Pour over the pickling liquid, making sure the fillets are covered, then cover with foil and pop into the oven for 10 to 15 minutes, or until the fish is just cooked.

9. Remove from the oven and allow to cool before transferring into a sealed container. Pop in the fridge when cool.

GRILLED SCOTTISH LOBSTER

WITH A WARM TOMATO & BASIL SALSA

Scottish lobster is renowned around the world. They are caught and landed all around the Scottish coastline, mainly by smaller local boats, and therefore they help support the local communities' economy. I get through dozens of lobster, per week, caught not far from the restaurant by one boat. Lobster is a real treat and surprisingly easy to cook and prepare.

MAKES 4 PORTIONS

For the lobster

2x lobster, around 1lb to 1⅓lb (450g to 600g) each

½ cup (120ml) white wine

1 carrot

½ leek

1 medium onion

1 lemon

6 white peppercorns

Small bunch parsley

1 bay leaf

For the salsa

1 tablespoon (15ml) vegetable or olive oil

2 red onions, finely diced

4 cloves garlic, crushed

Splash of white wine vinegar

3½oz (100g) ripe cherry tomatoes

Small bunch basil leaves, shredded

Small bunch cilantro, shredded

Salt and pepper

For the lobster

1. Your first task is to pop your lobster into the freezer. The idea behind this is that you want to put the lobster to sleep before it is put into the pot. We do this for two reasons: one is obvious – we do not want the lobster to suffer; second, if it is asleep when cooked, the lobster gives you a much better and more tender meat, as it does not tense up when hitting the water.

2. Choose a large pot and fill it with water to three-quarters full and bring to a simmer. Add all other ingredients and infuse for 10 minutes.

3. Now add the lobster to the pot and cook at a gentle simmer for 5 to 6 minutes. Take off the heat and allow to cool in the liquid.

4. Once cool, remove the lobster from liquid, take off the claws and split the lobster in half.

5. Clean out the head cavity, making sure you get the sack out from behind the eyes and discard, and also make sure you remove and discard the waste tract that runs down the tail.

6. Remove the meat from the tail and thinly slice, then pop the sliced meat back in.

7. Remove the meat from the claws and place in the cleaned cavity of the head.

For the salsa

1. Heat the oil in a medium-sized pan. Add the red onion and cook for 2 to 3 minutes.

2. Now add the garlic and cook for a further 30 seconds, then deglaze the pan with the white wine vinegar.

3. Next add the cherry tomatoes and cook for 5 to 6 minutes until they start to break down.

4. Add the shredded basil and cilantro, and check the seasoning.

To finish

1. Preheat your broiler, as hot as it will go.

2. Place your halved lobsters onto a tray, drizzle with a little oil and pop them under the broiler until they are nice and hot.

3. You can either spoon your salsa on top or serve it on the side.

OYSTERS

We are lucky that Scotland's waters are clear and cool, creating the perfect environment to grow oysters. They are cultivated in mesh bags on metal trestles on the sea floor; it takes three years for an oyster to reach its full size.

I always try and get Scottish oysters onto the menu when I am doing events promoting Scottish fish and shellfish, and have even had the help of Patrick McMurray (aka 'Shucker Paddy', the Guinness World Record holder for shucking oysters).

Opening an oyster is not for the faint-hearted. This will take practice and the most important thing is to avoid hurting yourself. You will need a thick kitchen towel and a proper oyster knife. Do not attempt this with a kitchen knife, as it's almost guaranteed that you will end up in the hospital. Another thing is that an oyster should be shucked just before it's consumed to preserve its freshness.

When opening an oyster, cover your hand with a towel and hold the oyster down firmly. Protecting your hand with a thick kitchen towel or cloth, you should insert the knife into the 'hinge' of the shell; this will take a bit of a push, but make sure the point of the oyster knife is in the shell before you twist it to open and cut under the oyster to release it. Give it a little sniff, as it should smell like the sea and be very pleasant.

There are loads of ways to serve oysters. Below are a few of my favorites.

- **Simple lemon juice:** a little squeeze on each.

- **Tabasco sauce:** this is the ultimate flavor explosion. The hot sauce works amazingly well with oysters.

- **Cocktail sauce:** take 2 tablespoons of tomato ketchup and mix with 1 teaspoon of horseradish sauce, and finally mix in 1 teaspoon of Worcestershire sauce.

- **Shallot vinegar:** this is always a popular choice. Take 1 shallot and finely chop it. Add Scant ¼ cup (50ml) of sherry vinegar, a little pinch of salt and pepper, and a pinch of white sugar. This is perfect.

GLEN ETIVE, THE HIGHLANDS

MEAT & GAME

RACK OF LAMB

WITH SMOKED CHEDDAR CRUST

This recipe is a real classic. There is nothing more indulgent than a rack of lamb. It is very similar to a dish I did on *MasterChef: The Professionals*. The best bit, in my opinion, is the wonderful cheese crust – if you use a mature smoked cheese, the flavor it adds is incredible. When buying the lamb, ask your butcher to French-trim it.

MAKES 4 PORTIONS

1 bunch of flat-leaf parsley, washed and stalks removed

4 cups (200g) fresh breadcrumbs

7oz (200g) smoked Cheddar cheese, grated

Good oil

1x 7 bone rack of lamb, French-trimmed

4 sprigs thyme

4 sprigs rosemary

Scant 2 tablespoon (25g) Dijon mustard

1. Your first task is to make the cheese crust. This can be done the day before, if you wish. Place the picked and washed flat-leaf parsley into the food processor and turn it to full power until the parsley is chopped.

2. Next, add the breadcrumbs and the grated cheese and blitz until you get a soft and bright green dough.

3. Take a chopping board, cover with plastic wrap all the way around, place your ball of green dough on top of the plastic wrap, and then cover the dough with more plastic wrap.

4. Using a rolling pin, roll out the dough until it is nice and thin; you should be able to cover the full board. Once that is done, place the board into the fridge and allow to set.

5. Next, heat a large frying pan on the stovetop. Add a little oil and pop the rack of lamb, skin side down, into the oil and slowly brown the fat. At this stage you are looking to render down the fat and crisp it up. Halfway through the browning stage, add your thyme and rosemary.

6. Once the skin and fat have achieved a good color, start browning the sides of the rack. Once done, set aside and allow to cool.

SERVING TIP

This is delicious served with gratin potatoes (page 44) and roasted vegetables (page 172).

7. When the lamb is cold, you are ready to cover it with the cheese crust. To do this, brush some of the Dijon mustard over the top of the lamb, then remove the top layer of plastic wrap from your crust.

8. Place the lamb rack skin side down onto the crust and then cut round the lamb to make a perfect covering.

9. You are now ready to cook the lamb. Preheat the oven to 350°F (180°C). Times will vary, depending on the size of your lamb and the performance of your oven. It will be much quicker than you think: 20 to 25 minutes is a good estimate. I use a temperature probe to obtain the perfect pink lamb; I tend to cook it to a core temperature of 128°F (53°C).

10. Once cooked, remove the lamb from the oven and set aside to rest. This process is vital. Rest the meat for 15 to 20 minutes, then carve.

PAN-SEARED LOIN OF VENISON

WITH RAW-SPICED CAULIFLOWER, BLACKBERRIES & GAME CHIPS

Out of all the dishes in the book, this dish is the one I have cooked the most. It was also my main course in the critics round of *MasterChef: The Professionals*. For me, this dish has huge impact and lots of texture and flavor. It will always have a special place for me and I'm so happy to have it included in this collection.

The great thing with this dish is that you could make all of it in advance and reheat when needed. All you have to do is sort out the cooking of the venison. For the game chips, you will ideally use a French mandolin, but a regular one will do just fine; use the latter to cut little discs out of the potatoes.

MAKES 4 PORTIONS

For the pan-seared loin of venison

4x 5oz (150g) venison loin
Scant 2 tablespoons (25ml) good oil
2 sprigs rosemary
2 sprigs thyme
1 bulb garlic
Scant ½ cup (100g) butter
1 pint blackberries, halved

For the raw-spiced cauliflower

½ medium cauliflower
Generous 1 tablespoon (20g) coriander seeds
½ cup (20g) chives
Salt and black pepper

For the pan-seared loin of venison

1. Marinate your venison in a little of the oil and half of the herbs for at least 3 hours and up to overnight.

2. When ready, preheat the oven to 350°F (180°C). Meanwhile, sear the venison in a hot non-stick pan, along with the other half of the herbs and 2 slightly crushed garlic cloves.

3. Once you have achieved lots of color on the outside, around 5 to 10 minutes, reduce the heat, add the butter and baste.

4. Remove from the pan and finish in the oven for 4 to 6 minutes, depending on size.

5. Allow the meat to rest before cutting.

For the raw-spiced cauliflower

1. In a dry pan, roast the coriander seeds until the room fills with their wonderful smell.

2. Transfer to a food processor and blitz, then add the cauliflower and blitz again until it looks crumbly and a little bit like couscous.

3. Remove from the food processor and season to taste. Mix in the chopped chives and set aside until needed.

recipe continues on the next page

For the caramelized cauliflower

½ cauliflower

2 sprigs rosemary

2 sprigs thyme

½ bulb garlic

Generous ⅓ cup (85g) butter

1 sheet parchment paper, cut into a circle just bigger than your pan

For the oats and nuts

⅓ cup hazelnuts (50g)

1 cup (100g) rolled oats

1 shallot, chopped

Scant 2 tablespoons (25g) honey

Scant 2 tablespoons (25g) butter

2 sprigs rosemary

2 sprigs thyme

For the game chips

2 good frying potatoes

Scant ¼ cup (50ml) oil for deep frying

For the caramelized cauliflower

1. Break the cauliflower into florets, cut each floret in half and place them flat side down in a non-stick pan.

2. Add the herbs, garlic and half the butter.

3. Cover with the circle of parchment paper and cook the cauliflower slowly on the stovetop. The idea behind this is that as the butter melts, the buttermilk will boil and steam the cauliflower, and as it evaporates the clarified butter then caramelizes the cauliflower. Add the remainder of the butter, if needed.

For the oats and nuts

1. Roast the hazelnuts in the oven at 325°F (160°C) for 5 minutes.

2. Remove the skins in a dry cloth, then blitz in a food processor to break them down a little, but not too far, as you want to leave some texture.

3. Place the nuts, oats, chopped shallot, honey, butter and herbs onto a baking tray.

4. Bake in the oven at 325°F (160°C) for 10 to 12 minutes.

For the game chips

1. Wash the potatoes. Cut them into thin slices in the gaufrette section on the mandolin.

2. Using a 1⅓in (35mm) cutter, press out little disks from the slices.

3. Deep fry the potato disks at 350°F (180°C) until golden brown and crispy.

To assemble

Reheat the caramelized cauliflower and carve the venison. Arrange the spiced cauliflower, nuts and oats on the serving plates, top with sliced venison, caramelized cauliflower and blackberries, and add the game chips on the side.

BRAISED VENISON & RED WINE STEW

I am a huge fan of braised food. Anything long and slow and jam-packed with flavor works for me every time. The working muscles in animals develop loads of flavor, due to the fact that they are always moving. They need a little care and attention, and a little more time to cook, as they tend to be tougher. The important part of this recipe is to make sure that you have a nice hot pan and you caramelize the meat well before adding any wine or stock. Loads of flavor is developed at this stage in the dish.

MAKES 4 PORTIONS

Scant 2 tablespoons (25ml) good oil

Salt and pepper

1lb (450g) venison haunch, trimmed and diced

Scant 2 tablespoons (25g) butter

2 shallots, diced

3½oz (100g) carrot, diced

½ leek, diced

2oz (50g) pearl onions

3 sticks celery, peeled and diced

3 cloves garlic, crushed

3 tablespoons (25g) all-purpose flour

2 tablespoons tomato paste

½ cup (120ml) red wine

1¼ cup (300ml) beef stock

3 sprigs thyme, fresh

1. For this you will require a saucepan with a lid, suitable for the oven. If you do not have one, you can follow the recipe using a pot and then transfer everything into a casserole dish and pop it in the oven. It will also work in the slow cooker.

2. Heat a teaspoon of oil the pan.

3. Season the meat and add to the hot pan. Make sure you do not add too much meat at a time, as you need to keep the pan hot throughout the browning stages. Color evenly for 4 to 5 minutes, then remove the meat from the pan and place to one side.

4. If necessary, add a splash more oil to the pan and then add the butter and slowly start to sweat the shallot, carrot, leek, pearl onions and celery.

5. Once softened, add the garlic and cook for 30 seconds. Now add the flour and tomato paste and cook for a minute.

6. Add the wine and reduce until fully evaporated, then add stock and the thyme.

7. Finally add the meat back into the pan and bring to a simmer.

8. Place the lid on the pot and put it into the oven at 300°F (150°C) for 1 to 2 hours or until the meat is tender.

WARM WOOD PIGEON

WITH BLACK PUDDING SALAD

Pigeon is one of the most underrated game birds in Scotland. It is abundant and available the whole year round. When I was a young chef, it was always on the menu – perfect for quick cooking and it works well with big flavors like balsamic and black pudding.

MAKES 4 PORTIONS

Generous ⅓ cup (85g) Puy lentils

Scant 3 tablespoons (40ml) good oil

3½oz (100g) bacon, diced

Salt and pepper

4 breasts wood pigeon

7oz (200g) black pudding

1 package mixed salad leaves

1 tablespoon (15ml) nice balsamic vinegar

1. Cook and cool the Puy lentils, as per package instructions.

2. Preheat the oven to 350°F (180°C).

3. Meanwhile, heat a non-stick frying pan with a teaspoon of oil, then add your diced bacon. Cook for 3 to 4 minutes over medium heat until golden in color. This will give the whole dish an incredible flavor. Remove from the pan for later.

4. Pour off some of the fat from the pan, season the pigeon and add to the hot pan.

5. Sear the pigeon well on both sides for 2 minutes each, remove from the pan and pop onto an ovenproof tray. Place in the oven for a maximum of 2 to 3 minutes. Take out and allow to rest. Resting is vital, as it allows the juices in the meat to settle and it will also even out the color of the meat.

6. Using the same frying pan, cook the black pudding for a minute on each side. Place into the oven for 2 minutes to make sure it is cooked, if necessary.

7. Now warm the lentils in the same pan and add the bacon back in.

8. Dress the salad leaves with a drizzle of balsamic and oil, crumble in the black pudding, lentils and bacon, and place in the center of a bowl or plate.

9. Slice the pigeon and place on top.

BREAST OF WOOD PIGEON

WITH CARAMELIZED RED ONION, BARLEY & BEETS

This is a very quick and simple recipe. Marrying pigeon with beets is a real classic combination. I like the addition of barley, as it adds a lot of texture to the dish and it also reminds me of evening walks in the summer where I live, watching the barley grow.

MAKES 4 PORTIONS

½ cup (100g) barley, soaked and cooked

Oil

1 red onion, finely diced

1 red chilli, finely diced

4 cooked beets, sliced (I use a few different types when I make this)

Scant ¼ cup (50ml) red wine vinegar

Salt and pepper

¼ cup (50g) sugar

8 pigeon breasts

Handful of mixed dressed leaves

1. Your first task is to soak and cook the barley. This can be done in advance.

2. Preheat your oven to 350°F (180°C).

3. Heat a pan on medium heat and add a splash of oil, then add the diced onion and chilli, and sweat until softened but without color.

4. Add the sliced beets and cook for a minute.

5. Add the red wine vinegar, turn up the heat and reduce by three-quarters.

6. Add the sugar, turn the heat down to a simmer and cook until the sugar creates a nice syrupy texture, approx. 7 to 8 minutes.

7. Season and set aside but keep warm.

8. Heat a non-stick pan, add a splash of oil, then seal the pigeon breasts on all sides, making sure you get a nice golden color on them.

9. Place into the preheated oven for 4 to 5 minutes. I think pigeon is best served pink. Once out of the oven, allow to rest for 2 to 3 minutes.

10. Slice the pigeon into two along the breast.

11. Arrange the warm beets onto each plate, along with some of the cooking juices and the cooked barley, then place the pigeon meat on top with a few dressed leaves.

ROAST LOIN OF RABBIT

WITH ROAST BABY CARROTS & SHALLOTS, HAZELNUT MOUSSE, CARROT & APRICOT PURÉE

We have a real abundance of wild rabbit in Scotland. They only enter the food chain as a result of land control in Scotland – and some people are very squeamish when it comes to trying something like it – but in Europe they specifically farm rabbits for food.

Rabbits have two very different types of meat: the loins, and the legs and the shoulders. Both require two very different ways of cooking. In this recipe we are going to concentrate on the loins. They are very tender and you need to take a lot of care when cooking them. I have been making this recipe for years; it works amazingly well as an appetizer.

We are only using the loins in this recipe, but as most people buy rabbits whole, I have a brilliant recipe for the rest of the rabbit on page 129.

MAKES 4 PORTIONS

For the loin of rabbit & hazelnut mousse

2 whole rabbits

Good oil

2 sprigs rosemary

2 sprigs thyme

¾ cup (100g) hazelnuts

2 sprigs dill

2 chicken breasts

1 egg

Scant ⅔ cup (150ml) whipping cream

½ package chives, chopped

½ package baby spinach

8oz (240g) pancetta or Parma ham (very thinly sliced)

Butter, for basting

recipe continues on the next page

For the loin of rabbit & hazelnut mousse

1. Bone out the rabbit by firstly removing the head, shoulders and legs. Put all of them to one side for another use, like the recipe on page 129.

2. Carefully remove the loins from the saddle and take away all skin and sinews, then marinate the loins with some of the oil and the rosemary and thyme.

3. To make the hazelnut mousse, place the hazelnuts in the oven at 350°F (180°C) for 4 to 5 minutes. Once roasted, remove their skins and blitz in a food processor until they look like breadcrumbs. Set aside.

4. Next, prepare the chicken. Remove and discard all sinews and skin from the breast. Blitz in a food processor with the egg, making sure to mix at top speed for at least 1 minute.

5. Transfer to a large bowl and fold in the whipping cream, hazelnuts and chopped chives.

6. To double check the seasoning of the mousse, take a small spoonful and pop it into a cup half filled with water and microwave for a minute or two to cook it. Let it cool slightly and taste, then adjust the seasoning if needed. Put the mix into a piping bag and put it into the fridge until ready to use.

For the carrot & apricot purée

1lb (450g) carrots

⅓ cup (50g) chopped
  dried apricots

Scant 2 tablespoons (25g)
  butter

Salt and pepper

For the roast baby carrots & shallots

8 baby carrots

Scant ¼ cup (50g) butter

1 sprig thyme

1 sprig rosemary

6 small shallots, halved

Good oil

7. Preheat the oven to 350°F (180°C).

8. Lay out a square of aluminum foil and place the pancetta flat on the foil. Pipe three thin lines of mousse mix onto the pancetta.

9. Cover the rabbit loin in baby spinach. Lay the spinach-covered loin on top of the mousse, then pipe the mousse on the sides and on top, covering the loin.

10. Roll the rabbit up in the foil, one round twist in the foil at the ends, one side toward you and the other away from you. Once twisted, push the ends in. This should give you a very round sausage shape. Do the same with the other loin.

11. To cook, place into the oven for 15 minutes until cooked.

12. Allow the meat to rest. Once ready to serve, remove from the foil and pan fry in oil (with a garlic clove and some hard herbs such as rosemary, bay leaves, sage and thyme if you like). Baste with a little butter to finish.

13. Slice each sausage into 4, allowing two slices per portion.

For the carrot & apricot purée

1. Wash, peel and rewash the carrots, dice and place into a pot of seasoned water.

2. Bring to the boil and cook until almost done.

3. Add the dried apricots and cook until the carrots are ready.

4. Pass through a colander, making sure to keep any liquid.

5. Place the carrots and apricots into the food processor with the butter and blitz until super smooth. Add more liquid, as you need it.

6. Keep warm.

For the roast baby carrots & shallots

1. In a large pan on high heat, add the carrots, herbs and butter.

2. Once the carrots have achieved some color and have softened, turn off the heat.

3. Next, halve the shallots through the circumference, keeping the skin on. Put the cut side down into a frying pan with a little oil.

4. Place onto the stovetop on medium heat and caramelize the bottom of the shallots.

5. Serve the roasted carrots and shallots alongside the carrot and apricot purée, and the roast loin sausage slices, and enjoy.

RABBIT STEW

This recipe is brilliant for using up the legs and shoulders of wild rabbit (perfect if you have any leftover from the roast loin of rabbit recipe on page 127). Wild rabbit can sometimes be a bit tough, so a long and slow cooking method is perfect.

MAKES 4 PORTIONS

1 leek

1 white onion

4 carrots

4 stalks celery

Scant 2 tablespoons (25ml) good oil

2 rabbits: bones, legs, shoulders and trimmings only

½ bulb garlic

4 sprigs rosemary

4 sprigs thyme

2 bay leaves

1 quart (1 liter) brown chicken stock (store-bought carton stock works well for this)

7 tablespoons (100ml) whipping cream

Small bunch tarragon, chopped

Small bunch dill, chopped

Salt and pepper

1. For this recipe, we are going to use half of the vegetables in the long, slow cooking stage of the dish and the other half to finish it off.

2. Cut half of the vegetables roughly and place into a large pot on low heat with a little of the oil and slowly caramelize.

3. Meanwhile, preheat the oven to 350°F (180°C). Place the rabbit bones, legs and shoulders into the oven and brown for 10 minutes.

4. Once you have achieved a good color on the vegetables, add the garlic and the herbs.

5. Next add the stock and bring to the boil.

6. Remove the rabbit from the oven and add it to the stock. Reduce the temperature of the oven to 300°F (150°C).

7. Place the lid on top of the large pot and pop into the oven for 1½ hours.

8. Meanwhile, finely dice the other half of your vegetables.

9. Remove the pot from the oven, and then the rabbit from the pot and set aside. Strain the cooking liquid into a wide-bottomed pan and bring back to the boil until the liquid has reduced by half.

10. Whilst the stock is reducing, remove the meat from the legs and shoulders and dice.

11. Once you have reduced the stock, add the whipping cream and the diced vegetables. Reduce again until you get a coating consistency and the vegetables are cooked.

12. Add the diced rabbit meat, tarragon and dill.

13. Double-check the seasoning and enjoy.

ROAST GROUSE

Grouse is a significant bird in the culinary world, and more so in the world of shooting. The season for red grouse starts on the 12th of August – known as the Glorious Twelfth. From a chef's point of view, this is a big day. Some of the finest kitchens in Scotland have competed with each other to see who could get a grouse on the table first. We actually have four types of grouse in Scotland, but it is the red grouse that is most commonly known. It has a far gamier flavor compared to most birds.

You'll notice that the method instructs you to roast the grouse on top of a bed of vegetables. The theory behind the vegetables on the bottom of the tray is to keep the grouse off the tray, and they also catch the cooking juices that can be turned into a roast gravy. This would pair exquisitely with roast potatoes, a recipe for which you'll find on page 172.

2 whole grouse

Salt and pepper

5oz (150g) dry cure bacon or pancetta

Scant ¼ cup (50ml) good oil

2 carrots, diced

2 sticks celery, diced

1 onion, diced

4 cloves garlic

4 sprigs rosemary

7 tablespoons (100ml) water

1. The first thing you need to do when roasting any bird is to make sure that it is free from feathers and stubble. Pick off any of the bigger feathers by hand and if you have a gas hob carefully hold the bird over the open flame to remove the fine hair and feathers. If you don't have a gas hob, a kitchen blowtorch works just as well.

2. Have a look and remove any bits and bobs from the inside – sometimes you might find a bit of lung stuck to the rib cage, so try and take away anything that is within the cavity.

3. Turn the bird around to the neck end, open up the skin flap and make sure that there is no food or grain stuck in the neck cavity.

4. Next, season the bird inside and out, then cover the breast meat with your bacon. The bacon's job is to protect the breast meat as it cooks; it helps retain moisture and slows down the cooking, as the rest of the bird takes longer than the delicate breast meat.

5. Using a bit of string, tie the legs of the grouse together and bring the string around the breast to pull the legs into the side of the bird. This also protects the breast meat and helps hold your bacon in place.

6. Preheat your oven to 350°F (180°C).

7. Heat up the oil in a frying pan on the stovetop and, once hot, brown the grouse.

8. Place your chopped vegetables into a roasting pan with the cloves of garlic and the rosemary, add the water to the bottom of the pan and then place the bird on top.

9. Pop the tray into the oven and cook for 35 to 45 minutes. Take time to baste the bird. If the liquid dries up, add more water.

10. You can tell if it is cooked when the shoulders of the bird are firm to the touch. It is best served pink.

SCOTCH PIE

The Scotch pie – affectionately known in Scotland just as a pie – has roots going back more than 500 years. It is probably best known for its popularity on a Saturday afternoon at football matches around the country. You can totally understand why it works: it can be eaten one-handed and it can also fit into your pocket – very handy, especially when you need to get back to your seat with a hot cup of Bovril. Incidentally, this is also a Scottish invention, originating with a butcher called John Lawson Johnston in 1874.

Scotch pies are normally made by bakers and butchers; the largest producer of them in Scotland is a company called Bells. Amazingly, Bells make so many pies every year that if they were stacked on top of each other they would be sixty-two times taller than Mount Everest.

They are very easy to make and are good fun. To make the pies you will need four molds, which you can easily pick up online. It is very satisfying to make them yourself, and if you are not in Scotland this is an amazing substitute.

For the hot water pastry

1½ cups (225g) all-purpose flour

Pinch salt

Scant ½ cup (100g) lard or butter, diced

½ cup (120ml) hot water

Whole milk

For the filling

Good oil

1 medium onion, finely chopped

Pinch nutmeg

4 sprigs fresh thyme

½ teaspoon black pepper

Generous ⅓ cup (85ml) lamb or beef gravy

8oz (225g) lean ground lamb or beef

For the hot water pastry

1. Sift the flour and salt into a bowl and make a hole in the center with your fingers.

2. Dice your lard or butter into small cubes and place in a pan with the hot water.

3. Heat the pan and stir until the fat has melted and mixed into the water. Pour this liquid into the hole in the flour and, using a spoon, combine the ingredients into a dough.

4. Once all the liquid has been used up, you can tip the mix onto the table and knead with your hands until you get a smooth and stretchy dough.

5. Push the pastry into a flat circle, wrap in plastic wrap and pop into the fridge to rest.

6. Once rested, roll the pastry out on a flat, floured surface.

7. Cut a circle of pastry about 8in (20cm) in diameter and carefully line the inside of your first pie mold.

8. Use a knife to trim the pastry to fit as needed. Repeat the rolling, cutting and trimming for the remaining three pie molds.

9. With the remaining pastry, cut four circles the same size as your molds and cut a small hole in the center of each.

10. Place the molds and pastry lids into the fridge for 30 minutes until the pastry hardens up.

For the filling

1. Preheat your oven to 300°F (150°C).

2. Place a little oil in a pan and add the onion. Cook over a low heat, stirring from time to time, until it is translucent and has a soft texture.

3. Stir in the nutmeg, thyme and freshly ground black pepper. Allow to cool.

4. Place the cooled onion into a deep bowl and add the gravy. I have used a ready-made version for this.

5. Add your ground lamb or beef and stir thoroughly to mix the ingredients.

6. Remove your pie shells from the fridge and spoon the meat into the pastry until they are about two-thirds full.

To assemble

1. Place the pie lids on top of the pies, lightly pushing the lid down onto the filling so there is a ¼in (½cm) deep rim around the top of each pie.

2. Brush the pies with a little milk.

3. Place on a flat baking tray and bake in the oven for 45 to 50 minutes until golden brown.

PHEASANT

WITH MUSHROOMS, PEARL ONIONS & TARRAGON

Pheasant is an iconic and beautiful bird, introduced in the UK as early as the eleventh century by the Normans. Originally from Asia, they can now be found all over the world. Pheasant is found on menus across Scotland. I spent a number of years working for the largest feathered game producer in Scotland, who has been instrumental in getting the birds from shooting estates all over the country and northern England onto the plates of hungry customers. This made birds such as pheasant a reliable and plentiful product. They can only be shot between the 1st of October and the 1st of February.

For this recipe, I have taken inspiration from a dish called chicken chasseur, or hunter's chicken. It is a one-pot wonder and helps the pheasant cook without drying out.

MAKES 4 PORTIONS

1 pheasant, prepared for cooking

Salt and pepper

Scant 2 tablespoons (25ml) good oil

Scant 2 tablespoons (25g) butter

3½oz (100g) pearl onions

3½oz (100g) bacon

7oz (200g) button mushrooms, trimmed and wiped

⅓ cup (50g) all-purpose flour

Scant ⅔ cup (150ml) white wine

Scant ¾ cup (200ml) beef stock

1x 14oz (398ml) can chopped tomatoes

3½oz (100g) cherry tomatoes, halved

Small bunch tarragon leaves

Juice of ½ lemon

1. Preheat oven to 325°F (160°C).

2. Cut the pheasant into four pieces, splitting the legs into thigh and drumstick and cutting the breast in two. Season with salt and pepper.

3. Heat a sauté pan with the oil, then add the butter. Once foaming, add the seasoned pheasant pieces, adding the thigh and drumsticks first.

4. Sauté over a reasonably high heat, turning and allowing pieces to become golden in color. Add the pearl onions and the bacon, and allow to color.

5. Remove the pheasant from the pan and place to one side. Pour off any excess fat.

6. Place the pan back on the hob and add the mushrooms. Cook until you have achieved some color.

7. Next, dust in the flour, making sure you stir it in until there are no lumps.

8. Now add the white wine and bring to the boil.

9. Reduce by three-quarters, then add the stock and reduce by half.

10. Add the canned tomatoes, cherry tomatoes and the tarragon.

11. Pop the lid back on and place into the oven for 1 hour. If you don't have a pan that works for the oven, you could pour the mix into a large casserole dish and cover with foil.

12. Season with salt and pepper, and finish the sauce with a squeeze of lemon juice to enrich its flavor.

MEAT & GAME

139

PAN-SEARED VENISON SALAD

WITH BEETS, WALNUTS, BROCCOLI & TARRAGON, & DUCK-FAT POTATOES

This is a surprisingly easy and earthy dish. It's incredible how the fresh tarragon and the balsamic vinegar completely lift the flavors.

MAKES 4 PORTIONS

For the pan-seared venison

1½lbs (675g) venison loin, trimmed and cut into 4

Scant 2 tablespoons (25g) butter

1 package pre-cooked beets (usually 4 beets)

1 head broccoli or broccolini, blanched

Scant 2 tablespoons (25ml) good oil

2 teaspoons balsamic vinegar

Salt and pepper

3 sprigs tarragon, chopped

½ cup (50g) walnuts, chopped

3½oz (100g) mixed leaves

Duck-fat potatoes

4 large potatoes, peeled and cut into your desired shape

9oz (250g) duck fat

2 sprigs thyme

2 cloves garlic, kept in the skin and slightly crushed

> Cut your potatoes into whatever shape you like. I used an apple corer to shape them.

For the pan-seared venison

1. Heat a non-stick pan. Rub a touch of oil and salt and pepper onto the venison, then add to the pan and sear well all over.

2. Reduce the heat and add the butter and a little splash of balsamic. Keep the venison moving in the pan and baste with the hot butter and vinegar.

3. After a few minutes, the venison will start to firm up. Turn off the heat and allow the meat to rest.

4. Meanwhile, cut each beet into 6 or 8 wedges or slices. Cut the blanched broccoli into little florets, trying to keep the natural shape of the vegetable.

5. In a small bowl, add the oil, balsamic and some salt and pepper. Next, add the beets and broccoli, then mix in the chopped tarragon, walnuts and mixed leaves. Season to taste.

6. Carefully arrange onto your plates or bowls. Slice the venison and place on top. Finish with your potatoes.

Duck-fat potatoes

1. Preheat your oven to 350°F (180°C).

2. In a pan, add the duck fat and begin to warm it up.

3. Next, add the potato, thyme and garlic.

4. Place the pan into the oven and cook until the potatoes are golden. Their shape determines the time it takes to cook; you'll know they're done when they are easily pierced with a knife.

HOMEMADE BLACK PUDDING

This is another fantastic recipe – one that was developed at college for student culinary competitions. As you can guess, chefs don't make black pudding day to day; we normally source it from a butcher. But I told my good friend and colleague Gordon Wallace, who is a master butcher, that I would like to learn how to make it and he let me pick his brain one day. This recipe was developed from that afternoon's conversation.

Like most of my recipes, this one is super simple. The dried blood you can easily pick up online (you can get a bag that makes four batches for a few pounds), the same is true for the natural sausage skins. I also have a builder's cement pointing gun that I use to fill the skins, which makes life much easier! I have made this recipe a lot over the years. It even made an appearance on *MasterChef: The Professionals* in a round called 'Showstopper'.

1 medium onion

5oz (150g) pork fat

2oz (55g) dried pig's blood

10oz (275g) suet (store-bought works well)

1¼ cup (125g) oatmeal

3 tablespoons allspice

1 tablespoon fennel seeds

1 tablespoon salt

5 tablespoons black pepper

2 cups (500ml) whole milk

1 natural sausage skin, salted

Probably the most famous pudding in Scotland is the Stornoway Black Pudding – it has even been granted Protected Geographical Indication (PGI) status.

1. The first task is to dice your onion and your pork fat.

2. Next, in a large bowl add your dried blood, chopped onion, suet, oatmeal, diced pork fat, allspice, fennel seeds, and salt and black pepper. You are probably thinking that this is a lot of pepper but each time I make it I tend to add more and more.

3. Give all of this a good mix. Now all you need to do is add your milk. I tend to do this a bit at a time until I have a runny, almost split-looking mix.

4. Depending on what skins you use, what you need to do to them will be different. I use natural skins that come in a plastic tube, and these need to be soaked and washed in cold water before use. Take your skin and tie a knot at one end; next, fill the skin. I use my builder's pointing gun for this; you could use a piping bag.

5. Fill the skin, but leave about 3in to 4in (8cm to 10cm) at the end, as this allows the pudding room to expand. Next push out as much of the air as possible and tie a knot at the other end.

6. Now, on to cooking. I have found through trial and error that this is better gently poached, so fill a large pan with cold water, roll your black pudding into a spiral and place into the water. Gently bring up to the boil, reduce the temperature and simmer for 20 minutes.

7. Once cooked, allow to cool in the cooking liquid.

8. Once cool enough to handle, chill completely in the fridge.

9. You can now use your black pudding in loads of different ways or simply broil it and eat it for breakfast.

FORFAR BRIDIE

As a youngster, I only knew the word 'Forfar' because of these amazing pastries, which I loved. I didn't even know it was a place. These savory delights are still very popular – I have a good friend, Laura, from Forfar, and every time she goes home to visit family I insist she brings back some bridies.

This recipe is good but it can't compete with the real thing, and if you get up to Forfar look out for them. One family baker in the town, JAS McLaren & Son, has been making them since 1893: five generations on and the same family are still there. A traditional Forfar bridie is made from short pastry. If you purchase one from outside Angus, you tend to find that it is made with puff pastry. I have used the traditional short pastry variant, but if you prefer puff pastry, buy some pre-rolled and follow the same steps. I have also made them a bit smaller, as Forfar bridies are huge – 8in (20cm) long at the straight edge!

MAKES 4 PORTIONS

For the pastry

1⅓ cups (200g) all-purpose flour

Good pinch of salt

Scant ½ cup (100g) butter, chilled

2 tablespoons (30ml) water

For the filling

1 tablespoon (15ml) good oil, plus extra for greasing

1 onion, finely chopped

1lb (450g) ground beef

1 teaspoon mustard powder

Generous ⅓ cup (85ml) beef stock

1 egg yolk, beaten

Salt and freshly ground black pepper

For the pastry

1. Sift the flour and the salt into a bowl.

2. Dice the chilled butter and add to the flour, lightly rubbing in the butter to achieve a sandy texture. Do this by running your hands down the insides of the bowl and go right to the bottom; when your fingers meet, slowly lift them out of the bowl, rubbing your thumbs over your fingers as you go. The secret of perfect pastry is to make sure you don't work it too much at this stage. I always try and make sure that I don't rub all the butter in completely. I like to see little flakes of butter once I have finished.

3. Make a well in the center of the flour and butter and add the water.

4. Gradually incorporate it into the flour and carefully bring together until you have a smooth paste.

5. Press into a flat round, wrap in plastic wrap and allow to rest in the fridge for 1 hour before using. The reason you press the pastry into a flat round is so that you can roll it straight from the fridge.

For the filling

1. Preheat the oven to 425°F (220°C).

2. Heat a frying pan until hot and add the oil and onion. Fry until golden and softened. Be careful not to burn it. Remove from heat.

3. Place the ground beef into a bowl with the mustard powder and beef stock. Once the onion has cooled, add to the mixture and season well with salt and freshly ground black pepper. Mix well to combine.

4. Roll out your short pastry (or puff pastry) on a floured surface until it is ¼in (5mm) thick, then cut out four 6in (15cm) diameter circles.

5. Place a spoonful of the mince mixture into the center of each pastry circle. Brush the outer edge of each circle with the beaten egg yolk.

6. Fold the pastry in half to create a semi-circle shape, and crimp the edges together well to seal. You can use a fork for this or your fingers.

7. Brush the pastry with the beaten egg yolk and season with salt and freshly ground black pepper.

8. Place onto a lightly greased baking tray and place into the oven to bake for 15 minutes.

9. Reduce the heat of the oven to 350°F (180°C) and cook for 30 minutes, or until golden brown and completely cooked through.

STEAK PIE

In our house, Hogmanay just wouldn't be the same without steak pie. My family traditions state that you eat steak pie just before the bells! I remember often racing home from a busy New Year's Eve night in the restaurant so that I could make it to my mother-in-law's in enough time to sit down and have this traditional feast. Most years I was late. Fast-forward a few years, and I teamed up with the biggest pie-maker in Scotland, Bells, and collaborated with them on their Hogmanay pies. As a result, my ugly mug adorns thousands of pies every New Year!

MAKES 4 PORTIONS

2lb (900g) stewing steak, cut into cubes

2½ tablespoons (20g) flour, seasoned with salt and pepper

2 onions, chopped

1 tablespoon chopped parsley

1 tablespoon chopped thyme

Salt and freshly ground black pepper

2 cups (500ml) beef stock, a quality cube will work for this.

8oz (225g) store-bought puff pastry

1 egg, beaten

1 tablespoon (15ml) good oil

1. Dust the cubed steak with the seasoned flour.

2. Heat some oil in a large heavy-bottomed pan and fry the meat, remembering not to shake the pan or to stir the meat until it has browned on that side. Browning meat is very important, as this is when you will create lots of flavor.

3. Once the meat has browned on all sides, add the chopped onions, herbs, salt, freshly ground black pepper and the stock, and bring to the boil.

4. Preheat the oven to 300°F (150°C).

5. Pop a lid on your pan and place into the oven until the meat is tender. This should take around 1 to 1½ hours.

6. Remove from the oven and increase the temperature to 375°F (190°C).

7. Transfer the filling mixture to an ovenproof dish.

8. Cut a piece of pastry and roll it out so it will fit across the top of the dish.

9. Whilst the pastry is still on the table, brush with egg yolk, then with the back of a butter knife make your chosen pattern.

10. Carefully lay the pastry over the dish and press the edges together to seal.

11. Make a small hole in the center of the pastry to allow the steam to escape.

12. Transfer to the oven and cook until the pastry is golden and crisp.

POTTED HOCK

I remember as a kid going to the local butcher's and buying potted hock for my dad. To be honest, I didn't have a clue what it was: it was set in a plastic tub and didn't look nice at all. Knowing what I know now, I wish I had bought two of them.

Most local butchers in Scotland will sell potted hock. It is thought that it originated in Glasgow. 'Hock' is the old Scots word for shin. Shin is a very tough cut of meat and takes a long time to cook, but your efforts will be worth it.

MAKES 4 PORTIONS

4lbs (1.8kg) beef shin, sliced

¼ teaspoon cayenne pepper

¼ teaspoon ground allspice

2 sprigs rosemary

3 sprigs thyme

1 bay leaf

Salt and pepper

Small bunch flat-leaf parsley, shredded

1. Place the beef shin, spices, rosemary, thyme and the bay leaf into a large pan and cover with cold water. Bring to the boil, then reduce the heat and let it gently simmer until the meat starts to fall off the bone. Throughout the cooking make sure you skim off the froth. This can take up to 6 hours!

2. Once cooked, strain the liquid into a separate pan and set aside to cool.

3. Remove all the meat and gelatinous fat from the bone.

4. Next shred the mixture as finely as possible and refrigerate.

5. Skim off the fat from the surface of the stock and return the shredded beef to the liquid. Season with salt and pepper to taste.

6. Bring this mix to the boil and simmer for a further 20 minutes. You should end up with what looks like a thick soup. Allow this mix to cool.

7. Next, add your shredded flat-leaf parsley and fold through.

8. You now need to set the mix into your molds or dishes: divide the mixture between them and refrigerate until set.

9. You can remove from the molds to serve or eat it straight from the dish on traditional oatcakes or hot toast.

LORNE SAUSAGE

Lorne sausage – or square sausage, as it is sometimes known – is hugely popular in Scotland but a bit of a mystery, not only in its origins but also in the fact that you never really know what you are going to get until you cook it. In some cases, it shrinks by half and all you are left with is a tray full of molten fat.

The origins of the name are also a mystery. A very famous Glasgow comedian called Tommy Lorne has been credited with being the source, but there is evidence that Lorne sausage was being sold in butchers' shops around the time he was born.

I think the most plausible explanation is that it is named after the Marquess of Lorne, as naming foods after famous people, especially aristocrats, was once very common. I am not sure how he would feel about a sausage being named after him . . .

MAKES 4 PORTIONS

1⅔ cups (100g) rusk or dried breadcrumbs

1 teaspoon ground black pepper

1 teaspoon salt

1½ teaspoons ground coriander

1 teaspoon ground nutmeg

Pinch nutmeg

½ cup (120ml) cold water

1lb (450g) ground beef

1lb (450g) pork sausage meat

1. You will need a 2lb (900g) loaf pan for this recipe. Put a little water into the bottom of the pan, then take three sheets of plastic wrap and place them inside (the water will help hold the plastic wrap in place).

2. Next place all of your dry ingredients into a large bowl and give them a good mix.

3. Add your water to this and mix together until you have a soggy paste, then add the beef and the pork sausage meat.

4. Give all of this a good stir. I find that if you use a gloved hand, you can get the mixing done better.

5. Next, take your mix and push it into the pan. Make sure you compact it as much as possible.

6. Once you have all the mix in the pan, cover with the plastic wrap and push it down.

7. Pop into the fridge or freezer until it firms up.

8. Once it has set, cut into ½in (1cm) slices and broil. Normally Lorne sausage is an integral part of a Scottish breakfast or served in a Scottish morning roll.

LAKE OF MENTEITH, NEAR STIRLING

VEGGIE & VEGAN

WARM PEARL BARLEY & ROASTED CARROT

WITH PICKLED SHALLOTS & DILL VINAIGRETTE

I just love barley; I watch it grow beside my house every year. It is a very versatile ingredient and adds a great texture to dishes. The combination of the roasted carrots and the pickled shallots give the dish a sweet and sour lift – it's just wonderful.

MAKES 4 PORTIONS

¾ cup (150g) pearl barley

Sprig of thyme

2 cloves garlic, crushed in the skins

Generous ⅓ cup (85ml) white wine vinegar

1 tablespoon coriander seeds

1 tablespoon black peppercorns

1 tablespoon yellow mustard seeds

Generous ⅓ cup (85ml) water

2 tablespoons (25g) sugar

A few sprigs of dill

7 tablespoons (100ml) good oil

3½oz (100g) shallots

10oz (300g) baby carrots, washed

Small handful spinach, shredded

1. The first task is to prepare the barley. Soak it in cold water for a couple of hours, then once it has softened rinse it in cold water. Pop it into a pan with the thyme and the crushed cloves of garlic, and some salt and pepper, and top it up with water. Bring to a simmer and cook until tender.

2. Once cooked, drain the water, spread out onto a tray and allow to cool.

3. Next, make the pickling liquid for the shallots. Pour scant ¼ cup (50ml) of vinegar, the coriander seeds, black peppercorns, mustard seeds, water and sugar into a pot. Bring to the boil, double check the balance; if it is too sharp, add a little water.

4. To make the dressing, chop the dill into a bowl, add the remaining Scant 2 tablespoons (25ml) of vinegar and generous ⅓ cup (85ml) of oil. Mix and season.

5. Meanwhile, peel and slice the shallots so that you get little rings and place them into the hot pickling liquid. Set aside.

6. In a large pan, heat a little oil and add the baby carrots. Pan roast them until they start to soften up.

7. Next add the cooked barley and heat through with the carrots, then the shredded spinach. Remove from the heat once the spinach has wilted.

8. Coat with the dressing and then top with the pickled shallots.

VEGGIE & VEGAN

155

GOAT'S CHEESE, ROASTED BEETS & CARAMELIZED WALNUT SALAD

Goat's cheese and beet is a classic flavor combination – one I used in the 'Chef's Table' episode of *MasterChef: The Professionals*. This salad looks great and everything can be done in advance, so it's a perfect dish if you are having people over for dinner.

MAKES 4 PORTIONS

1lb (450g) beets

Salt and pepper

2 sprig rosemary

2 sprig thyme

Scant 2 tablespoons (25ml) good oil

1 lemon

3½oz (100g) candy stripe beets

1 teaspoon honey

¾ cup (85g) walnuts

2 tablespoons (25g) sugar

5oz (150g) goat's cheese

1 small bunch chives, chopped

1. Preheat your oven to 350°F (180°C).

2. First, roast the beets. Cut into wedges, pop them into a bowl, season with salt and pepper, and add the rosemary and thyme, then coat with oil. Pour this mixture into a baking tray and place it the oven. The cooking time is going to be very different depending on the size of the beets. My advice is to set the timer every 10 minutes or so and keep checking. As you check, make sure you keep the ingredients moving on the baking tray.

3. Next, carefully peel a few thin strips from the lemon skin, remove the white pith and chop into thin strips. Juice the lemon.

4. For your pickled beets, thinly slice the candy stripe beets – this is best done on a mandolin, if you have one. Put the slices of beets and lemon zest into a pot with the honey and the lemon juice, and bring to the boil. Remove from the heat the second it comes to the boil and set aside.

5. For the candied walnuts, pop the walnuts and the sugar into a dry pan and place onto a medium heat on the stovetop. Keep the pan moving until the sugar starts to melt and caramelize. Remove from the heat and allow to cool.

6. Cut your goat's cheese into wedges.

7. You are now ready to plate your salad. To finish, dress with a little oil and some of the pickling liquid and chives.

ROASTED CARROT, SHALLOT & BEETS

WITH CARROT PURÉE & CHARD

This is a hearty dish with loads of flavor and textures. Cooking vegetables in different ways provides a different experience with every mouthful.

MAKES 4 PORTIONS

4 pre-cooked packaged beets

Salt and pepper

3 sprigs rosemary

3 sprigs thyme

Good oil

1lb (450g) carrots

2 cloves garlic

10oz (300g) small or baby carrots

4 banana shallots

2 handfuls Swiss chard, stalks and leaves separated

1. Preheat the oven to 350°F (180°C).

2. Cut the beets into wedges, place in a bowl, season with salt and pepper, add the rosemary and thyme, and coat with oil. Pour this mixture onto a baking tray and place it the oven. The cooking time is going to be very different depending on the size of the beets; check every 10 minutes or so until they're ready. Make sure you keep the ingredients moving on the baking tray.

3. For the carrot purée, wash, peel and rewash your large carrots, dice them and place into a pot of seasoned water. Bring to the boil and cook until tender. Pass through a colander, making sure to keep any liquid.

4. Place the baby carrots and some of the liquid into a blender and blitz until smooth. You may need to add more liquid to get the correct consistency.

5. Next, wash the baby carrots. I do not normally peel these, as the skins are perfectly edible.

6. Slightly crush the garlic cloves, but keep them in their skins.

7. In a large pan, add the carrots, garlic and some oil. Pop onto the stovetop and roast at a high heat.

8. Once the carrots have achieved some color and have softened, turn off the heat.

9. Halve the shallots lengthwise, keeping the skins on. Put cut side down into a frying pan with a little oil and place onto the stovetop on a medium heat to caramelize.

10. Once you have all your elements made, put the roasted baby carrots, shallots, beets and chard stalks into a pan and heat. Reheat the carrot purée.

11. Build your plates and top with the chard leaves.

BABY CARROT & CORIANDER SEED TART

Carrot and cilantro is such a classic combination. The cilantro I used in this recipe was from the community garden. It had just gone to seed and the seeds were still green – the blast of intense flavor that they gave was incredible. The only way you are going to replicate that exactly is to grow your own, but store-bought coriander seeds are worth a shot too!

MAKES 4 PORTIONS

1lb (450g) carrots
10oz (300g) baby carrots
2 cloves garlic
3 sprigs thyme
3 sprigs rosemary
Good oil
1 teaspoon coriander seeds
13oz (370g) puff pastry
1 egg yolk, for glazing

1. Your first task is to make a carrot purée. To do this, wash, peel and rewash your large carrots, then dice and place into a pot of seasoned water. Bring to the boil and cook until tender.

2. Pass the carrots through a colander, making sure to keep any liquid.

3. Blitz the carrots and some of the liquid in a blender and purée until smooth. You may need to add more liquid to get the correct consistency.

4. Next, wash the baby carrots. I do not normally peel these, as the skins are perfectly edible.

5. Keep the garlic cloves in their skins and slightly crush.

6. In a large pan, add the baby carrots, herbs, garlic and oil.

7. Pop onto the stovetop and roast at a high heat.

8. Once the carrots have achieved some color and have softened, turn off the heat. Remove from the pan and set aside.

9. Lightly toast the coriander seeds in a pan, then set aside.

10. Preheat your oven to 350°F (180°C).

11. Take your puff pastry, roll out to ¼in (½cm) thick and cut into rectangles.

12. Using the back of a butter knife, score a ½in (1cm) border around each rectangle of pastry. Next, pop them onto a non-stick baking tray or a baking tray lined with parchment paper. Brush with egg yolk.

13. Bake them in the oven until they puff up and turn golden brown.

14. Remove from the oven and push down the center between the cut border.

15. Spoon in a tablespoon of carrot purée, line up your carrots and top with toasted coriander seeds, then pop back into the oven to reheat.

CARAMELIZED CAULIFLOWER TART

WITH ONION PURÉE & CRISPY SHALLOTS

This is a vegetable-based dish that packs a real punch. The skill here is to caramelize the cauliflower to perfection; add to this the onion purée, and you've given a whole new dimension to the dish. You could make it any size you wish, from a party bite to a main dish.

MAKES 4 PORTIONS

3 medium onions

Good oil

4 sprigs thyme

1 bay leaf

1 medium cauliflower

4 sprigs rosemary

½ bulb garlic, skins on and slightly crushed

Salt

Generous ⅓ cup (85g) butter

13oz (370g) puff pastry

1 egg yolk, beaten

2 shallots

Scant ¼ cup (50ml) whole milk

¼ cup (25g) cornstarch

Oil for deep frying

Herbs of your choice or 4 green onions, sliced

1. First, make the onion purée. This is going to form the base of the tart and add moisture and huge flavor. Peel and finely slice the onions. Gently warm some good oil and a little splash of water in a pan, then add your onion, a sprig of thyme and the bay leaf. Season and cover with the lid.

2. Cook on a low temperature, but be careful not to color it. Once the onion is soft, remove the bay leaf and any thyme stocks and blitz in a food processor or with a handheld blender until smooth.

3. Break the cauliflower into florets. Cut each floret in half and place flat side down in a non-stick pan. Add a few sprigs of rosemary and thyme, crushed garlic, a pinch of salt and the butter.

4. Cover with a disk of parchment paper (cartouche) and carefully cook on a low heat until the cauliflower is caramelized.

5. Preheat your oven to 350°F (180°C). Take the pastry from the fridge. Roll out to ⅛in (½cm) thick, then cut the pastry into 6in (15cm) circles.

6. Using the back of a butter knife, score a ½in (1cm) border around each circle of pastry. Pop them onto a non-stick baking tray or a baking tray lined with parchment paper and brush with egg yolk.

7. Bake them in the oven until they puff up and turn golden brown.

8. Meanwhile, slice the shallots and separate the rings, dip into the milk and then the cornstarch and deep fry in hot oil until crisp.

9. To assemble the tarts, use one tablespoon of purée per tart and spread it over the base. Arrange the caramelized cauliflower and crispy shallots on top of the purée. When you are ready to serve, pop into a hot oven for 5 minutes to reheat. Finish with a sprinkle of fresh herbs or green onions.

ROAST SQUASH, MUSHROOM & OREGANO

Baby squash is more than a decoration; the flavor you get from these is amazing. Over the years I have roasted and filled these with lots of different things. The texture once baked is very rich and buttery. You will be able to find these in good fruit and vegetable stores in the fall.

MAKES 4 PORTIONS

4 baby squash
Salt and pepper
Good oil
1 butternut squash
7oz (200g) chestnut
  mushrooms
Small bunch chives
2 cloves garlic
Small bunch oregano
  leaves
1 zucchini

1. Preheat the oven to 350°F (180°C).

2. Cut the tops off the baby squash and remove the seeds, season the inside with salt and pepper, and rub them with some oil inside and out. Pop them into the oven. My squash took 20 minutes, but the timing depends on the size and age of the squash. You are looking for them to soften.

3. While they are roasting, peel and dice the butternut squash. Do this by halving the squash through the middle, so that you get a bulbous half and a straight half. You now have a flat edge that you can press down onto your chopping board. Peel it and chop it safely.

4. Place the diced squash onto a baking tray with some seasoning and oil, and pop it into the oven.

5. Next, slice your chestnut mushrooms and chives, then chop the garlic and half of the oregano leaves.

6. In a large pan, fry the mushrooms with the garlic and chopped chives and oregano.

7. Once the butternut squash is roasted, add it to the mushrooms and combine, then double-check the seasoning. Scoop this mixture inside the baby squash. Pop them back into the oven to keep warm.

8. Meanwhile peel and shred the zucchini using a grater, season and set aside.

9. Remove the filled squash from the oven, drizzle with a little oil and top with the shredded zucchini and the remaining oregano leaves.

BROCCOLI, BLUE CHEESE & BLACKBERRIES

This recipe uses the whole of the broccoli. The stalk is a fabulous ingredient in its own right; it has stacks of flavor and adds a different dimension to this dish. This recipe is jam-packed with ingredients that have loads of flavor and texture. It's also super simple to make.

MAKES 4 PORTIONS

1 head of broccoli

Generous ⅓ cup (85ml) white wine vinegar

Scant 2 tablespoons (25ml) honey

5oz (150g) blue cheese, diced

½ cup (85g) capers

1 handful of arugula

3½oz (100g) blackberries, halved

Scant 2 tablespoons (25ml) good oil

Salt and pepper

1. Prepare the broccoli by separating the stalk from the head.

2. Blanch the head of broccoli in boiling salted water for about 90 seconds, then cool immediately in cold water, drain and set aside.

3. Thinly slice the stalk and pop it into a pot with the vinegar and honey. I cut the slices with a round cutter just to make them look a little neater. Bring the vinegar and honey to the boil and immediately remove from the heat.

4. Break the blanched head of broccoli into florets and then slice.

5. You are now ready to build the salad. Place the sliced broccoli, cheese, capers and arugula into a bowl with the oil. Season with salt and pepper.

6. Divide the mixture between four plates and finish with the blackberries and the pickled broccoli stalks.

MUSHROOM, POTATO & LENTIL SALAD

This is my kind of food. Once you have all the elements sorted, you can get it all into a pan and finish it. The earthy combination of the potatoes, mushrooms and lentils really works with the dill pickle.

MAKES 4 PORTIONS

¾ cup (150g) green lentils
2 sprigs thyme
2 cloves garlic
10oz (300g) new potatoes
3½oz (100g) dill pickle
3½oz (100g) baby spinach
7oz (200g) mushrooms
Small bunch chives
Scant 2 tablespoons
  (25ml) good oil
Salt and pepper

1. The first thing you need to do is cook the green lentils. Place them in a pan and top up with water. Add the thyme and the garlic, and a little salt and pepper, put on the stovetop and bring to the boil. Once it comes to the boil, reduce the heat and simmer until the lentils are tender. Once cooked, drain the water off and allow the lentils to cool.

2. Meanwhile cook the new potatoes. Boil in salted water until tender, then again drain the water and let the potatoes cool naturally. Once cold, slice.

3. Slice the dill pickles, shred the spinach, quarter the mushrooms and chop the chives.

4. Place a large pan on the stovetop, add a little oil and, once hot, add the sliced potatoes. Fry until golden, remove and add the mushrooms. Cook until just browning.

5. Add the cooked lentils and warm. Next, add the pickle and the spinach.

6. Once the spinach has wilted, add the potatoes back in.

7. Finish with the chives and check the seasoning.

AVOCADO & GOLDEN BEETS

WITH A POACHED EGG

Beets are a brilliant ingredient and are relatively easy to grow. There are loads of different types that you can choose from. I have used beets a lot in my career in hundreds of dishes.

MAKES 4 PORTIONS

4 beets, red and golden varieties

2 sprigs rosemary

2 sprigs thyme

Scant ¼ cup (50ml) good oil

4 eggs

7 tablespoons (100ml) white vinegar

2 avocados

Juice of 1 lime

4 slices of bread, toasted

1 handful of arugula

Salt and pepper

1. Preheat your oven to 350°F (180°C).

2. First, roast the beets. Cut the beets into wedges, pop them into a bowl, season with salt and pepper, add the rosemary and thyme, and coat with oil.

3. Pour this mixture into a baking tray and place it in the oven.

4. The cooking time is going to be very different depending on the size of the beets. My advice is to set the timer every 10 minutes or so and keep checking. When you check, make sure you keep the ingredients moving around on the tray.

5. Next, poach the eggs. Take a medium pan of water and add a generous amount of vinegar. One small note to this: do not add any salt to the water, as the salt affects the egg white and breaks it down. Crack your eggs into four separate little cups or ramekins. To start cooking the eggs, take your little cup with the egg inside and slowly submerge the cup into the water. Once the cup is full of the hot water, carefully release the egg from the cup. By doing this the egg is not dropped in the water, therefore the yolk is surrounded in the white. Add all your eggs the same way. The other thing to note is that the water does not need to boil.

6. After a few minutes, the eggs should be ready. Remove from the water one at a time with a slotted spoon and submerge each one into ice-cold water to stop the cooking process. It also washes away the vinegar. Put the eggs to one side.

7. Next, halve the avocados and remove the flesh into a bowl. Season with salt and pepper, and add a squeeze of lime juice.

8. Reheat your poached egg in some simmering water. Meanwhile toast your slices of bread, top with the avocado, beets, arugula and poached egg.

ROAST POTATOES & VEGETABLES

Roast potatoes are the best thing ever. I have changed how I make them over the years and have simplified the process. In the past I have parboiled potatoes and roughed them up to get those lovely crispy edges. Now I just roast them from raw but with the addition of semolina. The semolina gives you a lovely crisp finish.

MAKES 4 PORTIONS

For the potatoes
4lbs (1.8kg) potatoes
(Yukon Gold or Red)
Generous ⅓ cup (85ml)
good oil
3 sprigs rosemary
3 sprigs thyme
½ cup (100g) semolina
Salt

For the vegetables
3½oz (100g) pearl onions
10oz (300g) baby carrots
5oz (150g) mushrooms
3 sprigs rosemary
3 sprigs thyme
Good oil
Butter
Salt and pepper

For the potatoes

1. Preheat your oven to 400°F (200°C).

2. Peel and wash the potatoes. Cut into even sizes.

3. Put in a bowl with the oil, herbs, salt and semolina, and give it a good mix.

4. Place onto a large baking tray, making sure that you give each potato some room.

5. Pop into the oven and cook until golden and soft. The time taken depends on how big you have cut the potatoes.

For the vegetables

1. First, prepare the vegetables. Wash and trim the onions and the carrots, and quarter the mushrooms.

2. Into a large pan, add the carrots and onions, oil and herbs. On a high heat, color and cook the vegetables.

3. Once they start to go soft, add the quartered mushrooms.

4. Once cooked, add the butter and double-check the seasoning.

RUMBLEDETHUMPS

Rumbledethumps must be the best name of any classic Scottish dish. It comes from how it is made – rumbled means mixed, and thumped means bashed, and that's exactly how it is made: by being mixed and bashed.

This is a super easy dish. It's basically a Scots version of the Irish colcannon. There is also a version using kale, called kale-cannon.

MAKES 4 PORTIONS

1lb (450g) potatoes (red work well for this)

1 small savoy cabbage or 2 bunches kale

2 medium onions, chopped

Scant 2 tablespoons (25g) butter

2 teaspoons salt

1 teaspoon black pepper

Small bunch chives, chopped

7 tablespoons (100ml) whipping cream

5oz (150g) smoked Cheddar cheese

1. Your first task is to wash and peel your potatoes, then cut them so that they are all of an even size. I find if you keep the potatoes large they cook better and are less starchy.

2. Place in a pan of cold water and add your salt, slowly bringing to the boil – this gives the whole potato a chance to heat up, and at the same time this stops the outside of the potato cooking first and overcooking by the time the inside is done.

3. Next, shred your cabbage. Bring a large pot of salted water to the boil and blanch the cabbage for about 90 seconds, then strain the water out and cool it immediately in cold water. Blanching and refreshing will help keep the cabbage nice and green throughout the cooking stages.

4. Take your chopped onion and pop in a pan with the butter and on a low heat soften.

5. Once your potatoes have cooked, strain through a colander and allow them to steam out for a couple of minutes.

6. Preheat your oven to 350°F (180°C).

7. Pop the potatoes back into the pot, add the onions, cabbage, salt, black pepper, chopped chives and whipping cream, and now rumbledethump them: stir and bash until all the ingredients have combined.

8. Next double check the seasoning and then pour into an ovenproof dish and top with the smoked Cheddar cheese.

9. Place into a hot oven for 30 minutes until the cheese is caramelized and golden.

HONEY-ROAST CARROTS

This is such a simple dish to prepare, and the flavor that develops when roasting vegetables is incredible. The addition of herbs and garlic in this recipe takes the carrots to new heights, but the real magic comes when the honey and the lemon juice are added. If you can't get a hold of baby carrots, regular carrots will work too, just chop them into large irregular pieces first.

MAKES 4 PORTIONS

1lb (450g) baby carrots
2 cloves garlic
3 sprigs thyme
3 sprigs rosemary
Oil
Scant ¼ cup (50g) butter
Scant ¼ cup (50ml) honey
1 lemon, juiced

1. Your first task is to wash the carrots. I do not normally peel baby carrots, as the skins are perfectly edible.

2. Keep the garlic cloves in their skins and slightly crush.

3. In a large pan, add the carrots, herbs, garlic and oil.

4. Pop onto the stovetop and roast at a high heat.

5. Once the carrots have achieved some color and have softened, reduce the heat.

6. Next, add the butter, lemon juice and honey.

7. Remove the herb stalks and garlic before serving.

BUTTERED KALE

Kale has become a superhero ingredient over the last few years; I have even started growing it myself. It's the plant that just keeps giving. Kale can be found everywhere now and is surprisingly tender – just don't overcook it!

MAKES 4 PORTIONS

2 bunches kale

Scant 2 tablespoons (25ml) good oil

Salt and pepper

2 cloves garlic

Scant ¼ cup (50g) butter

½ lemon, zested

1. Start by washing and tearing the kale. You want to remove and discard all the center spines.

2. Add the torn kale to a hot pan with the oil and some salt and pepper, and cook for a minute or so, then add the garlic, butter and the lemon zest.

3. Cook for another couple of minutes and serve.

VEGAN
Use non-dairy butter for a vegan alternative.

CAULIFLOWER CHEESE

Love it or hate it, cauliflower cheese is a staple not only in homes all across Scotland but also across the pond in North America. Cooked properly, this dish can be a masterpiece: Getting really nice high-quality cheese into the dish is a must, as is giving it a good blast under a very hot broiler so that you get the cheese nice and golden.

MAKES 4 PORTIONS

1 small onion

2 cloves

1 bay leaf

2 cups (500ml) whole milk

Scant ¼ cup (50g) butter

⅓ cup (50g) all-purpose flour

3½oz (100g) Cheddar cheese, grated

1 head of cauliflower, broken into florets

Salt and pepper

1. Make the white sauce. Peel your onion, then, using the cloves, pierce the bay leaf onto the onion. Place into a small pot and cover with milk.

2. Slowly bring the milk up to a simmer, then turn off the heat and allow the studded onion to flavor the milk.

3. Melt the butter in another small pan, then add the flour and mix to form a roux.

4. Cook out for 3 to 4 minutes, then slowly start to add the warm flavored milk. Stir continuously while the milk is added until you achieve a smooth sauce with the consistency of thick whipping cream. If you add the milk a little at a time, you will avoid making a lumpy sauce.

5. Cook this out for 10 minutes over a very low heat to avoid burning the sauce, stirring every minute or so.

6. Add half of the grated cheese, and double-check the seasoning.

7. Remove from the heat and cover with plastic wrap or parchment paper to avoid it skinning.

8. Meanwhile, cook your cauliflower in salted boiling water until tender.

9. Once cooked, refresh and cool in cold water, then drain as much of the water out as possible.

10. Preheat your oven to 400°F (200°C).

11. Arrange the cauliflower into an ovenproof dish, top with the sauce and sprinkle on the remaining cheese.

12. Pop into the oven until it is golden brown.

BEN NEVIS, NEAR FORT WILLIAM

BAKING & DESSERTS

RASPBERRY & HEATHER HONEY SORBET

This recipe makes the most wonderful sorbet/sherbet without the need for an ice-cream machine. The key to this is to freeze your fruit first and then blitz down the fruit in a blender or food processor. It is a brilliant way of enjoying summer fruit in the winter.

MAKES 4 PORTIONS

1½lbs (675g) frozen raspberries

1¼ cup (300g) natural yogurt

⅓ cup (100g) honey (I use heather honey in Scotland), plus more for garnish

1. Place the frozen raspberries into a blender or food processor. Blitz on full power for a few seconds until completely broken down. The fruit should be like a powder.

2. Next add the yogurt and the honey. Blitz until smooth.

3. Remove from the machine and pop into a tub; it might need an hour or so in the freezer before use. You can make this in advance and leave it in the freezer, but it will need to be put in the fridge to soften up for a couple of hours before serving.

RED BERRY & PEAR CRUMBLE

This is a fantastic method for making a real classic pudding. Adding some in-season red berries makes it really light and fresh. Cooking the fruit and the crumble mixture separately gives you a much better finish – I find if you cook the crumble on top of the fruit, you always get a stodgy bit in the middle and the fruit ends up overcooked. It also gives you a very crisp crumble topping.

MAKES 4 PORTIONS

For the filling

3 Bartlett pears, peeled and cut into cubes

¼ cup (50g) sugar

1 cinnamon stick

½ teaspoon lemon juice

10oz (300g) mixed red fruits

For the topping

Scant ½ cup (100g) butter, diced into cubes

Scant ½ cup (100g) superfine sugar

⅔ cup (100g) all-purpose flour

Pinch ground cinnamon

1. Add the pears, granulated sugar, cinnamon and lemon juice to a pot and simmer until soft. Remove from the heat.

2. Add the red berries whilst the pears are still warm. Mix once. Set aside in the fridge.

3. For the topping, add all of the ingredients together and rub with your fingertips until the mix resembles breadcrumbs.

4. Bake on a baking tray in the oven at 350°F (180°C) for 15 minutes, stirring every now and then, until the crumble is golden (please note: this crumble mix will not crisp up until it has cooled).

5. To finish the dish, place some of the fruit filling into each serving dish and top with the cooked crumble mixture. As everything has been cooked already, all you have to do is warm it up.

6. You can serve this with hot custard or vanilla ice cream.

GLUTEN-FREE & DAIRY FREE
This recipe works just as well with non-dairy butter and gluten-free flour.

GIN RED BERRY TART

For me, nothing says summer more than the start of the Scottish berry season – and gin!

Gin has been made in Scotland for more than 300 years and we produce some of the best-known brands in the world. In recent years, there has been a dramatic increase in its production here; its popularity has been the driving force of a great deal of new distilleries all over the country.

Scotland's soft-fruit production, too, has increased recently, doubling in the last ten years alone. Soft fruit from Scotland is very sweet: the more temperate climate here allows the berries to have longer daylight hours in summer but without high levels of heat. This allows the berries to ripen slower, so they produce more sugar and you get a sweeter berry.

I developed this recipe during the lockdowns of 2020 and made it for the first time live in front of hundreds of people via Facebook. It worked a treat! This tart is best done in the summer months when the fruit is at its best.

8x 4½in (11cm) sheets (vegetarian) gelatin

3½oz (100g) good quality chocolate

5oz (150g) shortbread

1⅔ cup (400ml) elderflower soda

7 tablespoons (100ml) gin of your choice

5oz (150g) strawberries

5oz (150g) raspberries

5oz (150g) blueberries

1. The first job is to bloom the gelatin. Do this by placing the gelatin into ice water to soften: use a bowl big enough so that you can submerge the sheets whole; do not break them up.

2. Melt your chocolate in a bowl set over a saucepan of simmering water. Be careful not to overheat the chocolate or get any water into it.

3. Crush your shortbread in a separate bowl, then add the melted chocolate and combine.

4. Line a 8in (20cm) tart pan with parchment paper. Press the shortbread and chocolate mix into the tart pan and place it in the fridge to set.

5. Next measure 7 tablespoons (100ml) of the elderflower soda into a small pot, bring to the boil.

6. Remove the gelatin from the ice water, making sure you squeeze out the liquid, then add the gelatin to the warm soda.

7. Stir the gelatin until melted, then add the remaining 1¼ cup (300ml) of soda and the 7 tablespoons (100ml) of gin.

8. Next, fill the tart with the fresh fruit, making sure you have a nice balance of different colors.

9. Carefully pour over the elderflower and gin mixture.

10. Place in the fridge until set.

TIPSY LAIRD

Researching recipes for tipsy laird has been fun. I have seen lots of weird and wonderful ideas for it. Most use raspberry jam, but for me when using a whisky liqueur I just find that jam is far too sweet and knocks the balance off. Most recipes also call for Amaretti biscuits and, as much as I think this would be a nice flavor, I am curious as to why an Italian biscuit would be a headliner in a Scottish dessert!

MAKES 4 PORTIONS

For the egg custard

1 cup (250ml) whole milk

Few drops vanilla extract

3 egg yolks

3 tablespoons (40g) sugar

1 orange, zest and juice

7 tablespoons (100ml) Drambuie

¼ cup (50g) sugar

1lb (450g) raspberries

1½ (350ml) whipping cream

12 ladyfingers biscuits (or Amaretti or sponge)

1¼ cup (300ml) custard, see recipe above

3oz (85g) flaked almonds, toasted

1. For the egg custard, place the milk and vanilla extract in a pot and bring to the boil.

2. Whisk together the egg yolks and sugar until frothy and lighter in color.

3. Take the milk off the heat and pour over the egg mixture while whisking continuously.

4. Transfer the mixture to a clean pot and place over low heat. Stir the mixture with a wooden spoon until the liquid coats the back of the spoon.

5. Place into a large bowl to cool.

6. Combine the orange zest and juice, 3½ tablespoons (50ml) of the Drambuie and 2 tablespoons (25g) of the sugar in a pot. Bring this mixture to the boil, then remove from the heat. Add just over half of your raspberries into the hot mix. Set aside.

7. In a large bowl, add the whipping cream and the last 2 tablespoons (25g) of sugar. Whisk until you start getting soft peaks. Be careful not to overwhip.

8. You can now start to build your trifle, either as one large tipsy laird or four individual ones. Place your chosen biscuits or sponge into the bottom of your dishes. Spoon the remaining Drambuie on top of your sponge. Next, layer the custard, the cream and raspberry mix. Top with some cream, fresh raspberries and the toasted flaked almonds.

ICED RASPBERRY & GLAYVA SOUFFLÉ

I first developed this recipe as a young chef for a small wedding I was doing. I wanted to get something as grand as a soufflé onto the menu but didn't have the confidence to put on a hot soufflé. The hardest thing about this recipe is getting the parchment paper around the outsides of the ramekin. Once you have sorted that it is a very easy dish to make. It is perfect for entertaining as it can be made well in advance. Before serving, I normally place the soufflés in the fridge for about 30 minutes to soften slightly.

MAKES 4 PORTIONS

1lb (450g) raspberries

Scant ¼ cup (50ml) Glayva liqueur

½ cup plus 2 tablespoons (150g) superfine sugar

1 cup (250ml) water

3 egg whites

Scant ⅔ cup (150ml) whipping cream

¾ cup (100g) chopped or slivered almonds, toasted

Confectioners' sugar, for dusting

1. You will need four ramekins for this. Wrap a strip of parchment paper around the outside of each ramekin, making sure the paper comes an inch (2½cm) above the top of the ramekin and secure with tape.

2. Place the raspberries and the Glayva into a food processor. Blend until smooth.

3. Pass the raspberry purée through a fine sieve into a bowl and set aside.

4. Place the sugar and water into a pan and gently heat until the sugar has dissolved, then bring to the boil and cook until the temperature of the mixture reaches 239°F (115°C). Check using a digital thermometer.

5. Meanwhile, whisk the egg whites until they form into soft peaks; this will be your meringue.

6. Once the sugar has reached the correct temperature, slowly pour the hot syrup into the meringue while whisking continuously.

7. Keep whisking until all of the sugar has been incorporated and the meringue is smooth and glossy.

8. Whip the whipping cream in a clean bowl until soft peaks form.

9. Pop your almonds onto a baking sheet and into the oven at 350°F (180°C) until golden brown. Set aside to cool.

10. Gently fold the whipped cream into the raspberry purée, and then fold in the meringue until just combined. Spoon the mixture into the prepared ramekins, bringing it up to the top of the parchment paper, then place into the freezer until set.

11. Once set remove from the freezer, take off the paper and roll the exposed edges of your soufflé in the baked cool almonds.

12. Dust with confectioners' sugar and serve.

APPLE CRUMBLE

Fruit crumbles have been a mainstay in Scottish cooking for hundreds of years, but it wasn't until the Second World War that they really took off, mainly because of a shortage of ingredients. Instead of flour, people could adapt and make a crumble with things like oats.

This recipe uses Braeburn apples, rather than traditional cooking apples. They are full of flavor and don't tend to break up too much during cooking. As they are naturally sweet, you don't need as much sugar.

MAKES 4 PORTIONS

For the apple mixture

3 Braeburn or Russet apples

1½ tablespoons (20g) butter

1 tablespoon (15g) soft dark-brown sugar

½ cinnamon stick

1 star anise

2 or 3 drops vanilla extract

Scant ¼ cup (50ml) cider

For the crumble topping

⅔ cup (100g) all-purpose flour

½ cup (50g) rolled oats

3 tablespoons (40g) sugar

Scant ½ cup (100g) butter, cut into cubes

Pinch of salt

Pinch of cinnamon

3 tablespoons (25g) hazelnuts, chopped

For the apple mixture

1. Peel, core, and cut your apples into quarters, and then cut each quarter again into four.

2. Heat a medium pan on the stovetop, add the butter and, as it starts to foam, add your cut apples. Cook for 2 minutes.

3. Add the sugar, cinnamon, star anise and vanilla. Stir gently to mix the flavors together. The sugar and the butter should start to caramelize.

4. Once the apples are golden, add the cider and gently simmer for 5 to 6 minutes or until the apples are nice and tender. Transfer to a baking dish.

For the crumble topping

1. Preheat your oven to 350°F (180°C).

2. Place the flour, oats and sugar into a bowl, add the butter and, with the tips of your fingers, gently rub it in to create loose breadcrumbs.

3. Add a tiny pinch of salt and cinnamon. Add the chopped hazelnuts and give it a good mix.

4. Spread the crumble on top of your cooked apple mix. Bake in the oven for 15 to 20 minutes or until the crumble is cooked.

CLOOTIE DUMPLING

I always remember my mum telling me stories of her mum's – my Nana's – clootie dumpling. Two things stuck out for me with this recipe: the first was that she added thruppenny bits (old 12-sided three penny coins) to the recipe. The idea was that each of the kids would receive a bit of cash in their slice of the pudding. I believe that the clootie dumpling could be filled with lots of different coins or charms all having a meaning to the finder. Second, my Nana did not work with a recipe – the whole thing was just judged by the eye and, most probably, using whatever was in the cupboard.

This recipe and method is based on what my mum passed to me. The word clootie is an old Scots word for cloth or rag. You will note at the end of the recipe it asks you to 'skin' the dumpling (which means to create a skin for it); this is a vital part of the process, and some people say it is not a clootie dumpling until it has been skinned. Traditionally this would be done in front of an open fire.

Additionally, for this recipe you will need a clean tea towel, two strips of parchment paper and some string. If you are going to add any coins or trinkets, make sure you wrap them in parchment paper.

4oz (125g) suet

1⅓ cups (200g) self-rising flour, plus 1 tablespoon for the tea towel

3 cups (150g) fresh breadcrumbs

¾ cup (85g) oats

Generous 1 cup (150g) raisins

Generous 1 cup (150g) currants

½ cup (100g) soft light brown sugar

1 teaspoon baking soda

1 teaspoon mixed spice

1 teaspoon ground ginger

1 teaspoon ground cinnamon

1 teaspoon salt

7 tablespoons (100ml) whole milk

2 tablespoons (30ml) light corn syrup

2 large eggs, lightly beaten

Egg custard (p. 192), for serving

To make your own self-rising flour, mix 1 cup all-purpose flour with 1½ tsp baking powder.

1. First, combine the dry ingredients: take a large bowl and add the suet, flour, breadcrumbs, oatmeal, dried fruit, sugar, baking soda, spices and salt. Give this a good mix until well combined.

2. Mix the milk with the light corn syrup and beaten egg.

3. Add the egg mixture to the dry ingredients and combine until you get a soft dough. You might need a little more flour if it is too sticky or a little more milk if it is too dry.

4. Take a tea towel and soak it in cold water. Squeeze out the excess water, lay the towel out onto a table, then lay two strips of parchment paper in a cross shape on the wet towel.

5. Generously dust the towel and the paper with flour. Place the ball of dough in the middle of the cross of the paper.

6. Bring the sides of the paper up over the dough. Cut any excess paper with scissors and cover the dough.

7. Next, bring the tea towel up over the dough and twist until it is tight. Tie with string.

8. Lower the dumpling into a pan of water and bring to the boil. Once the water comes to the boil, reduce the temperature and simmer the dumpling for 3 hours.

9. Once cooked allow to cool. Meanwhile preheat your oven to 350°F (180°C).

10. Unwrap the dumpling, place it on a baking sheet and pop into the oven for 10 to 15 minutes until the dumpling has skinned over.

BREAD & BUTTER PUDDING

This is one of those special dishes from my childhood. My mum did not make puddings very often, but she did make bread and butter pudding. Thinking back on it, I was never convinced it was actually anything close to being a dessert: plain bread with the crusts still on, and a custardy and butter mix. However, if you get the temperature correct and make sure you pack the dish with the custard mix, it can be a brilliant pudding. This dish is billed as a British classic – another recipe that is very thrifty, as it uses up stale bread, so it would have been popular during hard times.

MAKES 4 PORTIONS

10 slices white bread

Scant 2 tablespoons (25g) butter, plus greasing

2 eggs

Scant ¼ cup (50ml) whipping cream

1¼ cup (300ml) whole milk

5 tablespoons (60g) sugar

Pinch of cinnamon

⅔ cup (85g) raisins

Pinch of nutmeg

This recipe works well with non-dairy cream and milk and gluten-free bread.

1. Your first task is to get your bread buttered. Soften the butter, cut off and discard the crusts from the bread, then spread some of the butter over both sides of each piece.

2. Once buttered, cut each slice into 4 equal triangles.

3. In a bowl, whisk together the eggs, cream, milk and 4 tablespoons (50g) of the sugar, along with a pinch of cinnamon, then pop this custard into a jug.

4. Next, take some softened butter and coat a shallow oven-proof dish with it; this will stop the pudding sticking to the sides.

5. Layer the bread into your dish, then top with raisins, then pour on a little of the custard and allow it to soak up. Repeat this several times until there is a small pool of liquid in the bottom of the dish. It is vital that you let the bread soak up the custard.

6. Preheat your oven to 350°F (180°C).

7. We need to protect the pudding from direct heat in the oven, and to do this you will need a deep tray big enough that you can put your pudding dish into it. Pop the oven dish into your large, deep tray and pour in water to create a water bath (bain-marie), you want as much water as possible without flooding the pudding. This will allow the pudding to cook without scrambling the custard but also enable the top to become caramelized.

8. Sprinkle a little nutmeg over the top and your remaining sugar, then place the tray into the oven to bake for about 30 minutes.

9. Allow the pudding to cool before cutting.

BAKED RICE PUDDING

WITH DRAMBUIE

This is another dish from my childhood – except for the Drambuie, of course! It was a big hit growing up, and we would often have it with prunes. I still make it to this day, and it is my wife Sharon's favorite dessert. I have discovered if you use Arborio rice you get a fantastic texture and bite.

I know what you'll be thinking when you read through the ingredients list . . . and that will be: how can 2oz (50g) of rice and 2¼ cups (565ml) of milk work? But, trust me, it will. Please don't be tempted to add more rice! This recipe will also work well with non-dairy milk.

MAKES 4 PORTIONS

2oz (50g) risotto or pudding rice

2¼ cups (565ml) whole milk

⅓ cup plus 1 tablespoon (85g) superfine sugar

Scant 2 tablespoons (25ml) Drambuie

1 tablespoon (15ml) vanilla extract

Pinch of cinnamon

1 orange, zested and juiced

1. Preheat the oven to 300°F (150°C).

2. Rinse the rice in cold water to remove the dusty starch from the surface – this will prevent the pudding becoming too thick.

3. Place the drained rice in a large saucepan with the milk and about 2 tablespoons (25g) of sugar.

4. Bring to the boil, then turn the heat down and simmer very gently, stirring every few minutes for 15 minutes.

5. Simmer for 5 more minutes, stirring slowly all the time to prevent the rice from sticking to the bottom of the pan.

6. Add the Drambuie, vanilla, ground cinnamon and the zest and juice from the orange.

7. Pour into a shallow ovenproof dish. Bake in the oven for 30 minutes.

8. Remove the pudding from the oven and leave to rest for at least 1 hour – this will allow the creamy texture to develop.

9. Serve with some red berries or prunes.

CRANACHAN

This is another famous Scottish dessert. In fact, it is sometimes called the king of desserts. The origins of cranachan are actually rooted in it being eaten as a breakfast dish made from Crowdie cheese – a soft and fresh Scottish cheese made from skimmed cow's milk – combined with lightly toasted oatmeal, cream and local honey.

The word cranachan is Scottish Gaelic in origin, meaning 'churn'. It was originally a celebration of harvest, usually consumed with raspberries when they were in season, but now it is regularly served at Scottish dinners throughout the year.

I tend to keep it not too heavily mixed so that the individual ingredients can be tasted, and you should also be able to see each of the ingredients when it has been served. Another thing I found by accident is that heavy, smokey peaty whiskies work amazingly well in this dish. I discovered this when I was doing a small officers' mess dinner for the army at a very remote barracks on the west coast of Scotland and the only whisky I had was Laphroaig. It worked amazingly well!

MAKES 4 PORTIONS

¾ cup (85g) oats (rolled and steel cut both work well)

Scant ¼ cup (50ml) whisky

2½ tablespoons (50g) honey

2¼ cups (565ml) whipping cream

5oz (150g) raspberries

1. First, make the base for the dessert. To do this, place the oats in a dry pan and toast them. Once you get a little color, add the whisky – be very careful at his point as the whisky will ignite. Next, add the honey and remove from the heat. You need this mixture to cool to room temperature before it can be mixed with the cream.

2. In a bowl, whisk the cream into soft peaks. Try not to over-whisk it.

3. Once the oat mixture is cool, carefully fold in the raspberries and whipped cream, then spoon into serving dishes.

4. You can top with some honey and some more toasted oats and fresh raspberries.

BURNT CREAM

Burnt cream, aka crème brûlée. This dish has always intrigued me. I was once told that the French and the Scots have argued over the origin of this dish for centuries! One thing is for sure: this dish has been very popular in Scotland for a very long time.

I have included two methods for this: one oven-baked, the other cooked in the pan the whole way.

MAKES 4 PORTIONS

2¼ cups (565ml) whipping cream

1 drop vanilla extract

Peel of ½ orange

Pinch of cinnamon

6 egg yolks

Scant ½ cup (100g) superfine sugar, plus extra for the topping

Method One

1. Preheat the oven to 300°F (150°C).

2. Place the cream, vanilla extract, orange peel and a pinch of cinnamon into a thick-bottomed pot and slowly heat up.

3. Whisk the egg yolks and sugar together until the yolks lighten.

4. Remove the orange peel from the cream.

5. Stir half the warm cream to the egg yolk mix, then pour this mixture back into the pot.

6. Pour into ramekins, then place the ramekins into a shallow baking tray.

7. Carefully fill the baking tray with water.

8. Place the tray in the oven for 30 to 40 minutes, until they have set. They should have a little wobble but once cooled completely they will set. Place in the fridge until needed.

9. To create the crunchy caramel topping, sprinkle a thin layer of superfine sugar on top of the set cream. You have a couple of options on how to melt: I use a blow torch, but you can also use a brûlée iron, if you have one, or melt the sugar under a very hot broiler.

Method Two

1. Place the cream, vanilla extract, orange peel and a pinch of cinnamon into a thick-bottomed pot and slowly heat up.

2. Whisk the egg yolks and sugar together until the yolks lighten.

3. Remove the orange peel from the cream.

4. As the cream comes to the boil, add half the boiling cream to the egg yolk mix, then pour this mixture back into the pot and put back onto the stovetop.

5. You now have to be very careful. Keep stirring the mix until it starts to thicken. It should resemble thin custard.

6. Once it coats the back of the spoon, pour the mixture into a large jug or bowl. This instantly stops the cooking.

7. Pour this mixture into your ramekins. Once cool, place into the fridge to set.

8. To glaze, see step 9 to the left.

SCOTCH PANCAKES

WITH BLUEBERRIES & HONEY

Scotch pancakes – or drop scones, as they are sometimes known – are very similar to American pancakes. I am sure there must be a connection there. I make these at home with the kids; they just love all the mixing and mess, and then to drop the mix onto a hot pan and watch them rise is almost like magic.

MAKES 4 PORTIONS

1½ cups (225g) self-rising flour (see note on p. 201)

Pinch salt

¼ cup (50g) sugar

2 medium eggs

Whole milk – to make up to 1¼ cups (300ml) with the eggs

7oz (200g) blueberries

Honey, to serve

Butter, to serve

1. Sift the flour, salt and sugar together in a bowl.

2. Beat the eggs and milk, making sure you have made up the amount to 1¼ cups (300ml).

3. Slowly add the flour mixture to the eggs and milk, whisking as you go until you have a smooth, creamy batter. Most recipes state that you should add the liquid to the flour, but I feel it's much easier and less lumpy to do it the other way around.

4. Lightly grease a heavy-based frying pan or flat griddle pan and heat over medium heat.

5. To test the heat, put a teaspoonful of batter onto the pan. If it sizzles and cooks in less than a minute, it is ready.

6. Drop tablespoons of the batter onto the pan and smooth with the back of a spoon.

7. Cook until bubbles start to appear on the surface of each pancake. This will take about 3 to 4 minutes.

8. Flip the pancakes over and cook until firm and golden.

9. Keep the pancakes warm and repeat with the remaining batter.

10. Serve the pancakes hot with blueberries and honey and top with a knob of butter.

SEMOLINA PUDDING

I must admit, Scotland cannot claim semolina pudding as one of its own, but for many people my age it is something we fondly remember growing up with, from school lunches to having it at home. Semolina is a high-gluten wheat grain that is simply built with milk. In many ways it's very similar to rice pudding. I think the key to a good pudding is to get as much flavor into the milk as possible. You can infuse it with things like cinnamon, vanilla, citrus and cardamom.

MAKES 4 PORTIONS

2½ cups (565ml) whole milk

Few drops vanilla extract

1 cinnamon stick

2 to 3 cardamom pods

Generous ½ cup (100g) semolina

¼ cup (50g) sugar

5oz (150g) prunes

1. Heat the milk in a saucepan with the vanilla, cinnamon, and cardamom – crush the cardamom pods slightly to gain more flavor.

2. Bring to the boil, turn off the heat, then allow the ingredients to infuse and flavor the milk.

3. Once the milk is full of flavor, sift out the cinnamon stick and the cardamom pods.

4. Pop the milk back onto the stovetop and bring up to just before boiling. Add in the semolina and the sugar.

5. Reduce the heat and stir continuously until it thickens and is just starting to bubble. This should only take 5 to 10 minutes.

6. Serve with your choice of topping – prunes are a traditional choice.

This recipe will work well with dairy-free milk.

MORNING ROLL

This product is a truly local delicacy for me. I grew up in an area of Glasgow called Temple for a few years and our claim to fame was that the best roll on the planet was made a few hundred yards from my house. I am talking about the Mortons bakery in Glasgow.

Mortons opened in 1965 on Crow Road before moving to a new bakery in Drumchapel. I have a family connection to the bakery, as both of my younger brothers worked there in the late eighties. I looked forward to my dad picking them up after a night shift, as he always brought home the rolls that were straight from the oven.

I now wish I had managed to do a few shifts myself; I would love to have found out how they make them. I think they must be doing some sort of sourdough method, but I can't be sure. For me, a Mortons roll can stand side by side with any French baguette.

This recipe is the closest I can get to a Glasgow roll. It's not as good as the real thing, but it's worth trying if you can't get a true Mortons roll.

5⅓ cups (800g) white
   bread flour
2 teaspoons salt
2 cups (500ml) water
1 package (¼oz/7g) dried
   yeast
2 teaspoons sugar
Scant ¼ cup (50g) butter
¼ cup (50g) semolina

1. Your first task is to place the flour and salt into a large bowl and give it a good mix.

2. Next, measure your water. You are looking to get your water to 98°F (37°C) – that's baby bottle temperature. Add your yeast and sugar to the water.

3. Rub the butter into the flour and salt.

4. Once the butter is crumbled in, make a well in the center and add the water.

5. Slowly incorporate the flour and water together until you have a rough dough.

6. Tip your dough out onto a work surface and begin to knead. Use enough flour for kneading until you achieve a smooth dough. You can also use some of the semolina for the kneading process. This can take up to 15 minutes.

7. Place back in the bowl, cover with plastic wrap and allow it to proof until it doubles in size. The time it takes to do this depends on the temperature of your kitchen.

8. Once it has doubled in size, tip it out of the bowl and knead it for just a few minutes. This stage is called knocking back, the idea being that you are removing all of the large air bubbles.

9. Preheat your oven to 410°F (210°C).

10. Cut your dough in half and then cut each half into 5 equal balls. Next, roll the balls with your hand until they are round and smooth.

11. Using a rolling pin, flatten out the balls until they are about 1¼in (3cm) thick. As you roll, sprinkle a layer of semolina on top, making sure the rolling pin squashes it in a little.

12. Line your baking tray with parchment paper and sprinkle some of your semolina onto the paper.

13. Next, lay your flattened dough onto the parchment. Don't worry about the rolls touching as they proof, you want the rolls once proofd to join up at the edges.

14. Loosely cover with some plastic wrap and re-proof for 15 to 20 minutes or until the rolls have again doubled in size. Proofing should be quicker this time, as the yeast has been activated in the first proofing.

15. Bake for 16 minutes or until the rolls are golden brown.

16. Once cooked remove from the oven and cool on a rack.

TATTIE SCONES

A tattie scone is a breakfast delicacy in Scotland, served on the hoof, often found sandwiched in a crispy morning roll with a slice of Lorne sausage and a good dollop of ketchup. Equally, it can appear on breakfast menus in five-star hotels across the country.

Tattie scones are something most people would buy ready-made and they are normally bought from a local baker's. In saying that, they are easy to make at home; however, you do need to take care when cooking them. The best way to make a potato scone is in a griddle pan, though a flat frying pan can also be used.

MAKES 12 SCONES

9oz (250g) potatoes
Scant 2 tablespoons (25g) butter
Pinch salt
⅓ cup (50g) all-purpose flour
Good oil

1. Your first job is to boil the potatoes and then mash them thoroughly in a large mixing bowl. Traditionally, families would be using leftover mashed potato from the night before.

2. Add the butter and salt.

3. Add the flour with the mashed tatties, ensuring the mixture does not go dry. You might have to add more mash or flour to get the consistency correct. It should be almost like pastry.

4. Empty onto a flat surface and use a rolling pin to roll out the mixture evenly and to a thickness of about ¼in (4mm). Using a 8in (20cm) plate, cut into a circle and then into triangles. You could also cut them into smaller rounds; some bakers around the country sell round tattie scones.

5. Heat some oil in the griddle or frying pan – be careful not to use too much oil – then place each potato scone in the pan and cook on both sides until brown.

This recipe works just as well with gluten-free flour and non-dairy butter.

6. You can make these in advance and reheat or eat immediately.

OATCAKES

Very few things are more Scottish than oatcakes. Like a lot of traditional recipes, they are very simple to make. I have used this for many years and it always works; I even managed to incorporate it on an episode of *MasterChef: The Professionals*. Oatcakes were also the very first thing I ever tried to cook. I was around eleven years old and I attempted them without any recipe or understanding of cooking at all. In doing so, I managed to set my mum's kitchen on fire. I thought that if I spread some leftover breakfast rolled oats on a tray and popped them under the broiler, somehow, by magic, they would turn into oatcakes. They didn't! After that, I asked for some cookbooks for my birthday.

MAKES 12 LARGE TO 24 SMALL

3 tablespoons (25g) all-purpose flour

Pinch salt

Pinch baking soda

1¼ cups (125g) rolled oats (additional oatmeal is required for rolling out)

Scant 2 tablespoons (25g) butter

¼ cup (60ml) boiling water

1. Preheat the oven to 350°F (180°C).

2. Sift the flour, salt and baking soda into the oatmeal.

3. Melt the butter in the boiling water and add to the dry ingredients.

4. Mix until the mixture feels spongey.

5. Turn the mixture onto a surface scattered with oatmeal and scatter more on top of the dough.

6. Flatten it out and then roll with a rolling pin to ¼in (5mm) thick. Cut into circles.

7. Place the circles on a non-stick baking tray and bake in the oven for 15 to 20 minutes until golden.

PERKINS BISCUITS

Perkins biscuits – not to be confused with the Yorkshire biscuit Parkins (they are similar but not the same) – are worth a go if you like your biscuits with a bit of oaty texture. This is my type of biscuit – another very easy one to make and I think they look amazing. You could add your own twist; topping them with some dark chocolate would work well.

MAKES 24 BISCUITS

¾ cup plus 2 tablespoons (125g) all-purpose flour

1 teaspoon baking soda

½ teaspoon ground ginger

½ teaspoon ground cinnamon

¼ mixed spice

¼ cup (60g) butter, diced and cold

1¼ cups (125g) rolled oats

⅓ cup plus 1 tablespoon (85g) superfine sugar

⅓ cup (100g) light corn syrup

¾ cup (100g) blanched almonds

This recipe works just as well with gluten-free flour and non-dairy butter.

1. Preheat the oven to 350°F (180°C).

2. Take the flour, baking soda, ginger, cinnamon and mixed spice, and sift them into a large bowl.

3. Add the butter and rub until the mixture resembles breadcrumbs.

4. Add the oats and sugar and mix.

5. Take a small pan and warm the light corn syrup until it is of a pouring consistency – try not to heat it too much.

6. Pour the light corn syrup to the bowl and mix to form a stiff dough.

7. Line two baking trays with parchment paper.

8. Split the mixture in half and roll it into a long sausage shape.

9. Cut each sausage shape into 12 equal parts.

10. Roll each piece into a ball, split the balls between the two trays, leaving a gap between the balls.

11. Gently press the tops of your biscuits with your thumb and top each with a blanched almond.

12. Bake in your oven for 10 minutes until the biscuits have spread and are golden.

13. Leave to cool on the tray before transferring to a wire rack.

ABERNETHY BISCUITS

Surprisingly these biscuits are not named after the village of Abernethy in Perthshire but have been attributed to Dr John Abernethy, a specialist in digestive health who invented these biscuits as an aid to the digestive system. It was one of many digestive biscuits that were invented at the time.

These little biscuits are really simple to make, and they're perfect with a cup of tea. You can easily make them with gluten-free flour and non-dairy butter.

MAKES 12 TO 14 BISCUITS

1½ cups (225g) all-purpose flour, plus extra for dusting

½ teaspoon baking powder

¼ cup plus 2 tablespoons (90g) butter, diced and cold

¼ cup plus 2 tablespoons (90g) superfine sugar

½ teaspoon caraway seeds

1 tablespoon (15ml) whole milk

1 egg

Oil, for greasing

1. Preheat oven to 350°F (180°C).

2. Take a baking tray and, using a piece of paper towel, rub it with a little oil and then dust with some flour to make it non-stick.

3. Now to start the biscuits, sift the flour with the baking powder into a large bowl.

4. Rub in the butter with your fingers till the mixture resembles breadcrumbs.

5. Next mix in the sugar and caraway seeds.

6. Mix the milk and egg together and add to the mixture, then slowly knead together to form a dough.

7. Dust your work surface with a little flour, tip your dough onto the surface and roll out to ⅛ in (3 to 4mm) thick. Cut into 12 to 14 rounds. With this mix you should be able to re-roll the trimmings.

8. Place your cut biscuits slightly apart on the baking sheet.

9. Bake for 10 to 12 minutes until golden.

10. Allow to cool on wire rack.

AYRSHIRE SHORTBREAD

This recipe comes from a handwritten book that was sent to me from a family who wanted me to have their great-grandmother's recipes. Her name was Jessie Henderson and she was a student of the E. C. Training College in Edinburgh. This recipe is from her class notes dated the 3rd of June 1893. The collection is incredible – it was written in impeccable handwriting, and we are still teaching lots of these recipes today. It is my honour to share some of her recipes with you.

MAKES 12 SQUARES OR FINGERS

1 cup (225g) butter
1½ cups (225g) all-
   purpose flour
1⅓ cups (225g) rice flour
⅔ cup (125g) sugar
1 egg
2 tablespoons (15ml)
   whole milk

1. Rub the butter with the dry ingredients until the mixture is like breadcrumbs.

2. Beat the egg and add it to the milk, add this to the dry mix and combine until you have a soft dough.

3. Turn onto a floured surface and, with a floured pin, roll out thinly.

4. Cut into squares (or fingers), prick with a fork, then bake in a 'quick oven' at 350°F (180°C) for 10 to 15 minutes.

5. Remove from the oven and dust with sugar.

Ayrshire Shortbread

½ lb. flour   ½ lb. rice flour
½ lb. butter   ¼ lb. powdered
1 egg.   2. tablesp.

Rub butter with dry ingredi...
breadcrumbs — beat eg...
a soft dough. ...
pin roll o...
to f...

BUTTERIES

A buttery – or Rowie, or Aberdeen roll – reminds me a little of a French croissant. It is very rich and flaky. It is said to have been made for fishermen, as they needed something that could last longer than the more traditional bread; it is also jam-packed with fat, so provided loads of energy for the fisherfolk working hard out at sea.

When I think of butteries though, my main thought is of a chef who has been part of my career for more than thirty years, as teacher, employer and friend – Mr Willie McCurrach OBE. Being from Aberdeen, he is a true expert in the art of making butteries, and that is why it is his recipe that is below and not mine!

MAKES 15 BUTTERIES

3⅓ cups (500g) white bread flour

Scant 1 tablespoon (15g) salt

1 package (¼oz/7g) dried yeast, or ½oz (15g) fresh yeast (if you're able to find some!)

1¼ tablespoon (15g) sugar

1½ cups (350ml) warm water, at 98°F (37°C)

Generous 1½ cups (350g) butter, softened

1. Preheat the oven to 400°F (200°C).

2. Put the flour and salt into a mixing bowl and combine by hand. Add the yeast and sugar and give it a stir.

3. Next, measure the water. I find it easier to get a jug to the correct temperature and then measure it.

4. Make a well in the center of the flour and add the water. Using a spoon, mix the water and the flour to create a rough dough.

5. Pour this mix out onto a table and knead it until smooth.

6. Dust a bowl with flour, drop in the dough and cover with plastic wrap. Leave it to double in size.

7. When the dough is ready, knead it for a further 2 minutes to knock out the air. Doing this will ensure that you get an even rise in the final pastry.

8. Roll out into a rectangular shape, 8in x 16in (20cm x 40cm) approximately, and spread the softened butter onto two-thirds of the dough, fold the remaining third of dough over the butter and fold over again so the butter is fully enclosed.

9. Carefully roll it out again into a rectangle and fold again as before.

10. Divide the mixture into 15 pieces and mold into circular shapes. Place onto a greased and heavily floured heavy baking tray, and using a floured hand pat the rolls out. They should look rustic in shape.

11. Allow to proof for 20 minutes and bake for 15 to 20 minutes until dark golden brown.

SHORTBREAD

I am obsessed with keeping recipes. I love having a record of what I cook, so when writing a recipe my first source is my own files. This is a very simple recipe and, whatever source you find for shortbread, your recipe will probably be very similar to this one.

Shortbread has a long and noble history, dating as far back as the 12th century. It was originally made from leftover bread dough. It was said that Mary Queen of Scots was a big fan – she particularly liked petticoat-style shortbread.

For this, I have made traditional fingers and petticoats using a wooden mold. These can be bought online. (Word of caution: you do not bake the shortbread in the mold.)

MAKES 4 PORTIONS

Generous ½ cup (125g) soft butter

5 tablespoons (60g) sugar

1 cup plus 2 tablespoons (170g) all-purpose flour

¼ cup (25g) cornstarch

1. Preheat the oven to 325°F (160°C).

2. Using a wooden spoon, mix the butter and sugar together until pale and creamy.

3. Sift both the flour and the cornstarch into the bowl and mix well.

4. Turn the dough onto a lightly floured surface. Shake a little flour on top of the dough and roll out to about ¼in (5mm) thick.

5. You now have a choice of what shape to make them: you can use a shortbread mold or cut into round biscuits, roll into a rectangle and then cut into fingers or, even using a plate, cut into a circle. Whatever shape you decide on, you need to make your markings and prick with a fork before it goes into the oven.

6. Use a palette knife to lift the shortbread onto an oiled baking tray and bake for about 25 minutes until golden brown. Just be careful with your timings, as the shape you decide on will have an impact on the time it takes to cook.

7. When the shortbread is ready, remove from the oven and sprinkle some sugar on top whilst it is still hot.

8. Move your shortbread onto a cooling rack. Once cool, store in an airtight container.

BEREMEAL BANNOCKS

This is a fantastic recipe from the works of a Mrs Margaret B. Stout, who in 1925 published a book called *Cookery for Northern Wives*, written to document the traditional recipes of the people of Shetland. It was sent to me by her daughter, Margaret Stuart, as she knew I love the Shetland Isles. In fact, I was heading to Shetland a few weeks after I received the book, so I had an understanding of the traditional foods.

Bannock is a type of unleavened bread, traditionally cooked over the fire on a hot skillet. There are loads of different types of Bannocks found around Scotland. The word derives from the Gaelic "bannach" meaning morsel.

Beremeal is a flour made from a type of barley, and originates in Shetland, Orkney and the Western Isles. If you can't find beremeal where you are, use regular barley flour instead. Shetland bannocks are traditionally made on a griddle or stone in a peat fire. It is likely that these bannocks have been cooked there in this way for thousands of years, and they're as integral a part of Shetland culture now as ever.

MAKES 4 PORTIONS

3 cups (450g) all-purpose flour

1½ cups (225g) beremeal barley flour

1 teaspoon salt

1 small teaspoon cream of tartar

2 small teaspoons baking soda

2 cups (500ml) water

1. Sift all the dry ingredients together.

2. Add the water and mix to make a soft dough. Make it just as soft as can be easily handled.

3. Turn the dough onto a floured surface and gently roll out to ¾in (2cm) thick.

4. Cut into squares or rounds.

5. To cook, place a dry frying pan on the stovetop and heat up – to test the heat sprinkle some beremeal onto the pan and if it starts to color the pan is hot enough. Cook the squares or rounds on both sides for about 4 minutes, or alternatively bake in the oven at 350°F (180°C).

SELKIRK BANNOCK

A Selkirk bannock is a very sophisticated, luxurious tea loaf, once a favorite of Queen Victoria. Selkirk bannocks are still made in the Borders. I've used a traditional method in this recipe, which will take a bit of elbow grease, but it is worth giving it a go.

This wonderful little loaf was given a mention in the writings of none other than Sir Walter Scott in *The Bride of Lammermoor*.

MAKES 8 PORTIONS

For the batter

⅔ cup (100g) white bread flour

1¼ cup (300ml) warm whole milk, 98°F (37°C) (baby bottle temperature)

1 teaspoon sugar

1 package (¼oz/7g) dried yeast

For the dough

2⅔ cups (400g) white bread flour

1 teaspoon salt

Generous ⅓ cup (85g) butter

¼ cup (60g) superfine sugar

3 cups (400g) raisins

1 egg, to glaze

> This recipe works well with non-dairy butter.

1. Your first task is to make what is called a batter. Sift the flour into a large bowl. Warm the milk and add the sugar and yeast to it, giving it a whisk. Add this to the bowl with the flour and mix

2. Cover the bowl with plastic wrap and set aside. The idea is to activate the yeast, so after about 20 to 30 minutes you should see this mixture start to bubble.

3. Move on to the dough. Sift the flour into a large bowl and add the salt.

4. Next, rub in the butter and sugar until the mix resembles fine breadcrumbs.

5. Check on your batter; if it is activated, stir it into the flour and butter mix. Combine well to form a soft dough.

6. Turn the dough onto a lightly floured board and knead until smooth. It should bounce back when you press it.

7. Shape the dough into a round ball. Dust the sides of a clean bowl with flour and place the dough into it, then cover with plastic wrap. Set aside until it has doubled in size.

8. At this stage, knead in the raisins, working them through till they are evenly distributed. Don't worry that you are knocking out all the air.

9. Keep kneading the dough until it is smooth. Now shape the dough into a round bloomer-loaf shape

10. Place on a greased baking tray, cover with plastic wrap loosely and set aside to double in size. This could take up to 1 hour.

11. Meanwhile preheat oven to 350°F (180°C).

12. Once your dough is ready, brush with a beaten egg and bake for 50 minutes or until a skewer inserted into the center comes out clean.

EMPIRE BISCUITS

I always remember as a kid being told that empire biscuits were originally called German biscuits, and that the name was changed at the outbreak of the First World War. The name has stuck, and this biscuit couldn't be more Scottish: double shortbread, with raspberry jam and icing.

MAKES 4 TO 6 DEPENDING ON THE SIZE OF YOUR CUTTER

For the shortbread

⅔ cup (150g) butter, softened

⅓ cup plus 1 tablespoon (85g) superfine sugar

2 egg yolks

1 teaspoon vanilla extract

1⅔ cups (250g) all-purpose flour

For the filling and topping

Strawberry or raspberry jam to fill

Scant 3 tablespoons (40ml) whole milk

Scant 1 cup (250g) confectioners' sugar

10 glacé cherries

This recipe will work just as well with non-dairy butter and milk and gluten free flour.

For the shortbread

1. In a large bowl, cream the butter and sugar. I usually use a spoon but you could use a machine. We are looking for the butter to go light and fluffy and a pale yellow color.

2. Now add the yolks and the vanilla extract and work into the butter mixture.

3. Finally sift in the flour and bring it together to form a smooth paste.

4. Next, on your work surface, use the back of your hand to flatten out the dough. Wrap it in plastic wrap and pop it in the fridge to rest and firm up.

5. Once chilled, roll the dough out to ¼in (5mm) thick and using a pastry cutter cut out 8 to 12 circles of shortbread.

6. Place on a non-stick baking tray and pop back in the fridge to rest once again. Resting the dough will help stop shrinkage.

7. Bake at 325°F (160°C) for 8 to 10 minutes. The baking time will depend on the size of the biscuits.

8. When the biscuits come out of the oven, place on a wire rack to cool. Allow to cool completely before attempting to ice.

For the filling and topping

1. Start by selecting and pairing the biscuits so that all biscuits are matched with similarly sized tops and bottoms.

2. Next, decide which biscuits you intend to be bases and which you intend to be tops.

3. Take some of the jam and evenly spread onto the base biscuits, then firmly place the tops on.

4. With all the biscuits sandwiched with jam, place onto a wire cooling rack to glaze with the icing.

5. To make the icing, mix together the milk and the confectioners' sugar to create a solution that is smooth and that just pours off a spoon.

6. Glaze evenly and top with a glacé cherry while the icing is still soft.

FOCHABERS GINGERBREAD

There is a huge choice of different gingerbread recipes, and while writing this book I had to select which I wanted to use. It was an easy choice in the end, as I used this recipe on *MasterChef: The Professionals*. It was part of the appetizer dish I did for the 'Chef's Table' episode, so you might have an idea of the direction this recipe is going: it's not sweet or sickly but heavy, spicy and moist. Another reason I was drawn to using this in the first place was that it had almost half a bottle of beer in it!

MAKES 10 TO 12 SLICES

½ cup (110g) butter

½ cup plus 1 tablespoon (110g) sugar

⅓ cup (110g) molasses

1 egg

1½ cups (225g) all-purpose flour

1 teaspoon mixed spice

2 teaspoons ground ginger

1 teaspoon ground cinnamon

½ teaspoon ground cloves

1 cup (110g) mixed dried fruit

⅓ cup (40g) ground almonds

⅓ cup (40g) flaked almonds

⅓ cup (40g) candied peel, finely chopped

½ teaspoon baking soda

Scant ⅔ cup (150ml) dark beer

> This recipe works just as well with gluten-free flour and non-dairy butter.

1. Grease and line a 8in x 4in (20cm x 10cm) loaf pan with parchment paper. I find it easier if you brush the sides of the pan with a little oil first, as this helps the paper to stick to the pan.

2. Preheat the oven to 325°F (160°C).

3. In a bowl, cream the butter and sugar until light and fluffy, add the molasses and fold in.

4. Beat your egg in a small bowl and then gradually add it to the butter and sugar mix, beating well in between additions.

5. Sift the flour and spices into a clean bowl. Next add the dried fruit, almonds and candied peel. Add all of this to the butter mixture.

6. Next dissolve the baking soda in the beer, add to the mixture and combine.

7. Pour into your lined loaf pan and bake in the oven for 45 minutes to 1 hour. The way to test the cake to see if it is cooked is to press the top and if it bounces back, it is ready.

8. Once out of the oven, let it rest for 10 minutes, then turn it onto a wire rack to cool completely.

GINGER SNAP

I have a love-hate relationship with these little biscuits: I love the flavor of them, they are almost savory, and the strength and pepperiness of the ginger is brilliant; the reason I hate them is simply the name – being a redhead, as a kid more people called me ginger snap than Gary. Now everyone just calls me Garibaldi!

MAKES 12 LARGE TO 24 SMALL

2 cups (300g) all-purpose flour, extra for rolling

2 teaspoons ground ginger

1 teaspoon baking soda

½ cup (50g) fine oatmeal

Scant ½ cup (100g) butter, diced

Generous ¾ cup (170g) soft brown sugar

4 tablespoons (60ml) light corn syrup

1 egg

1. Preheat the oven to 350°F (180°C).

2. Sift the flour, ground ginger and baking soda into the mixing bowl. Add the fine oatmeal.

3. Using your fingers rub the butter it into the flour mix until crumbly.

4. Add the soft brown sugar, light corn syrup and egg, and mix well until it forms a firm doughy mixture.

5. Roll out the dough on a floured surface to about ¼in (5mm) thick. Using a cookie cutter, cut the dough to your preferred size (I like about 1½in (4cm) for small and about 2½in (6cm) for large). Place onto a non-stick baking tray.

6. Pop the tray into the preheated oven. Bake for 7 to 10 minutes until golden.

This recipe works just as well with gluten-free flour and non-dairy butter.

OVEN SCONES

I just love making scones. I'm also not bad at them, the reason being that I have listened to loads of great chefs and bakers for hints and tips on how to achieve the ultimate scone. Big things I have learned: that the addition of acid gives incredible lift, and that if you bunch them close together they create moisture between them and stay really light. There is nothing worse than a heavy scone.

Scones got their start as a Scottish quick bread. Originally made with oats and griddle-baked, today's version is made with flour and baked in the oven. As for the origin of the word *scone*, some say it comes from the Dutch *schoonbrot*, which means 'beautiful bread', while others argue it comes from the Stone of Scone, on which the Kings of Scotland were crowned. According to *Webster's Dictionary*, scones originated in Scotland in the early 1500s.

MAKES 10 TO 12 SCONES

Scant ⅔ cup (150ml) whole milk

½ lemon

2½ cups (370g) self-rising flour (see note on p. 201)

Pinch cinnamon

¼ cup (60g) butter, diced and fridge cold

¼ cup (60g) superfine sugar

¾ cup (100g) raisins

Milk, for glazing

1. First, sour the milk with the lemon juice. This creates a chemical reaction with the baking powder that is in the flour, giving you a much better lift, thus a lighter scone.

2. Preheat the oven to 350°F (180°C).

3. Sift the flour and the cinnamon together into a large bowl.

4. Carefully rub in the cold, diced butter.

5. Add the sugar and the raisins.

6. Tip the soured milk into the mixture and knead lightly.

7. Remove from the bowl and roll to a thickness of 1½in to 2in (4cm to 5cm) on a floured surface.

8. Use a crinkled cutter to shape your scones to the size you prefer, then put on a non-stick baking sheet. I find that if you bunch them relatively close together you get a better lift.

9. Brush with milk and cook for about 10 to 16 minutes, depending on size.

This recipe works well with non-dairy butter and milk.

DUNDEE CAKE

Dundee cake is arguably the most famous of all of Scotland's bakery recipes. Known as the Queen of Cakes, it was first made for Mary, Queen of Scots in the sixteenth century. The queen didn't like cherries, which were very popular at the time, so the local baker added almonds and a legend was born. This recipe also incorporates marmalade – another incredible Dundonian invention.

MAKES 10 PORTIONS

For the cake

¾ cup (100g) blanched almonds

Scant ¾ cup (170g) butter, soft

Generous ¾ cup (170g) light brown sugar

1 orange, zested

1 lemon, zested

3 tablespoons Dundee marmalade

1½ cups (225g) all-purpose flour

1 teaspoon baking powder

3 large eggs

¾ cup plus 1 tablespoon (100g) ground almonds

2 tablespoons (30ml) whole milk

2 cups (250g) raisins

2 cups (250g) currants

⅓ cup (50g) mixed peel

For the glaze

1 tablespoon (15ml) whole milk

2 teaspoons superfine sugar

This recipe works just as well with gluten-free flour and non-dairy butter and milk.

1. Put the whole almonds into a small bowl and pour over boiling water to just cover. Leave for 5 minutes, then drain and place into a clean cloth to dry.

2. Line a deep, loose-based 8in (20cm) cake pan with parchment paper.

3. Place your butter into a large bowl and beat well until soft. Add the sugar and beat until light and fluffy.

4. Stir in the orange zest, lemon zest and the marmalade.

5. Sift the flour and baking powder together.

6. Add the eggs to the creamed butter and sugar, a little at a time, beating well between each addition. If it starts to curdle, dust in a little flour.

7. Add the flour and ground almonds, and mix well.

8. Mix in the milk and then add the dried fruit and peel. Mix gently together.

9. Preheat the oven to 325°F (160°C).

10. Carefully spoon the mixture into your cake pan. Next, carefully, using the back of a spoon, flatten off the top mix so that it is nice and level.

11. Arrange the whole almonds close together in neat circles on the top of the cake to give you the iconic, traditional look.

12. Bake in the oven for 45 minutes.

13. Lower the oven temperature to 300°F (150°C) and cook for a further 60 to 80 minutes.

14. Check the cake after 50 minutes by inserting a metal skewer into the cake. When it's done, the skewer should come out clean. Check every 10 minutes.

15. When cooked, remove the cake from the oven.

16. Next you need to make your glaze. Put the milk and sugar into a small pan and heat gently until the sugar has dissolved.

17. Brush over the top of the cake and return the cake to the oven for 3 to 4 minutes.

BLACK BUN

The Black Bun – or, as it is sometimes known, the Scotch Bun – is traditionally eaten at Hogmanay and should be delivered by your first-footer at the bells, with a lump of coal and a bottle of whisky in hand. With me being short and ginger, I was never a welcome sight as a first-footer – a tall, dark-haired and handsome individual is the custom. Don't be put off with this huge recipe: it is worth the effort.

For the pastry

2 cups (300g) all-purpose flour

½ teaspoon baking powder

Pinch of salt

Generous ⅓ cup (85g) butter, chilled

3oz (85g) vegetable shortening

Generous ⅓ cup (85ml) cold water

1 egg, for glazing

For the Black Bun mix

Generous 1⅔ cups (250g) all-purpose flour

1 teaspoon baking soda

1 teaspoon ground ginger

1 teaspoon ground cinnamon

1 teaspoon ground allspice

1 teaspoon mixed spice

½ teaspoon black pepper

½ cup plus 2 tablespoons (125g) dark muscovado sugar

3 cups (400g) raisins

3 cups (400g) currants

1 cup (125g) chopped mixed peel

4 tablespoons (60ml) buttermilk

2 eggs

2 tablespoons (30ml) whisky

For the pastry

1. Sift the flour, baking powder and the salt into a bowl.

2. Dice the chilled butter and vegetable shortening and add to the flour, lightly rubbing them in to achieve a sandy texture. Do this by running your hands down the insides of the bowl and go right to the bottom; when your fingers meet, slowly lift them out of the bowl, rubbing your thumbs over your fingers as you go. The secret of perfect pastry is to make sure you don't work it too much at this stage. I always try and make sure that I don't rub all the butter in completely. I like to see little flakes of butter once I have finished rubbing in.

3. Make a well in the center of the mix and add the water. Gradually incorporate it into the flour and carefully bring it together until you have a smooth paste.

4. Cut the pastry into two – one piece a third of the total, the other two-thirds. Press both pieces of pastry into a flat round, wrap in plastic wrap and allow to rest in the fridge for an hour before using. The reason you press the pastry into a flat round is so that you can roll it straight from the fridge.

For the Black Bun mix

1. Preheat your oven to 325°F (160°C).

2. The first job is to sift the flour, baking soda and the spices into a bowl.

recipe continues on the next page

3. Add the remainder of the dry ingredients (sugar, dried fruit and peel) and mix well.

4. Next add the buttermilk, egg and the whisky.

5. Mix until you get a stiff and sticky mix. Set aside.

Assembling the Black Bun

1. Preheat the oven to 325°F (160°C).

2. Slightly oil or line your loaf pan with parchment paper. If you have a nice new pan, oiling it will be enough.

3. Roll out the two-thirds piece of pastry. Take your time and be careful not to use too much flour, as this can dry it out. Another thing to bear in mind is that the rolling pin should only be pushed backwards and forwards – you should turn the pastry and not the pin, as you get a much more even pastry that way and can guarantee that it isn't sticking to the table. The pastry is moving at every turn.

4. Make sure you roll the pastry big enough so that you will have an overhang, then lift and line the loaf pan with it. This pastry is very forgiving so it should be easy enough to do. Push the pastry into all the corners of the pan.

5. Next take your black bun mix and fill the pan with it, making sure you fill all the gaps.

6. Finally, roll out the remaining piece of pastry for the lid. Roll the same way as before until it is big enough, then brush the edges of the overhanging pastry with beaten egg. Carefully place the pastry on top.

7. You can now use your artistic flair to finish. Crimp the edges by pinching them with your fingers to create a seal.

8. To finish, brush the top of the bun with the beaten egg and bake for 2 hours.

9. Once cooked allow it to cool in the pan.

NORTH BERWICK BEACH

WEE TREATS

WHISKY CHOCOLATE TRUFFLES

I have been using this recipe my whole career. It has been a mainstay of my petit four repertoire. It is super luxurious and very easy to make. The chocolate ganache can be flavored with anything you wish – any type of liqueur works, as do things such as orange zest, dried fruit or pistachios. You can also use milk and white chocolate; however, you won't need as much cream.

MAKES 24 TRUFFLES

1¼ cup (300ml) whipping cream

Scant ¼ cup (50ml) whisky or whisky liqueur

Few drops vanilla extract

10oz (300g) dark chocolate, 53% cocoa or above

1¼ cup (100g) sweetened shredded coconut, toasted

2oz (50g) cocoa powder

1. The first task is to flavor the cream. To do this, add the whisky and the vanilla to the cream. Place it on the stovetop and heat it up.

2. In a separate bowl, break your chocolate into small bits.

3. Once the cream has come to the boil, pour it over the chocolate.

4. Stir until the chocolate has melted and the ganache is nice and smooth.

5. Pour the ganache into a container and once at room temperature place into the fridge to set.

6. Once set, you are now ready to roll the ganache into truffles. I do this with a melon baller. I find I get a very even, round truffle this way. You will need a cup of hot water to heat up the scoop before dipping it into the ganache, if you use this method. Alternatively, you can scoop out the ganache with a spoon and shape it with your hands.

7. Drop the ganache balls into the toasted coconut or cocoa powder.

8. You can re-melt the ganache and set it in the fridge and repeat the process. When you do so, be very careful not to overheat the ganache, as it will split.

WHISKY FUDGE

I don't consider myself as having a sweet tooth, but fudge is my downfall. This is a simple recipe and I find it much easier than making tablet. Be warned that this is a very hot mix, so be careful when making it. It also really helps if you have a thermometer to hand; if not, you can test the mix using what's called the 'soft ball' test. Drop a little of the mix into a bowl of water and if you can roll it into a little ball between your fingers, it is 'soft ball', meaning it's ready.

MAKES 10 PORTIONS

1x 14oz (398ml) can condensed milk

Scant ⅔ cup (150ml) whole milk

1lb (450g) light brown sugar

½ cup plus 1 tablespoon (125g) butter

Scant ¼ cup (50ml) whisky

Few drops vanilla extract

You will also need a 8in x 8in (20cm x 20cm) baking tray lined with parchment paper

WARNING
This mixture boils at a very high temperature. Be careful.

1. Mix together the condensed milk, milk, sugar and butter in a heavy-bottomed pan.

2. Place on a low heat and stir until the sugar has dissolved.

3. Turn up the heat and boil the mix, stirring constantly until it reaches 244°F (118°C) – what we call 'soft ball' consistency.

4. Take off the heat and continue to stir. Next, add the whisky and vanilla extract. Be careful, as the mix will boil up a little when the whisky is added.

5. Continue to beat until the fudge is no longer shiny and begins to thicken.

6. Pour the mixture into the prepared baking tray and spread level.

7. Set aside to cool to room temperature and allow it to firm up.

8. Once set, lift the fudge out of the baking tray and using a sharp knife slice it into cubes.

9. This is best stored in a sealed container.

TABLET

Tablet is one of the most famous sweeties to have come from Scotland. It was first mentioned in *The Household Book of Lady Grisell Baillie* written in the early 18th century, and has stood the test of time. Thanks to the Scots' sweet tooth (and it being easy to make at home) it's as popular now as it has ever been.

I have been making Scottish tablet for over 30 years. I was first taught the recipe by one of Scotland's great chefs, Nick Nairn. This is a variation on his brilliant tablet recipe. Nick never told me why he included vinegar in the recipe, so I am not 100% sure what benefit it gives the recipe, but all I know is it's by far the best tablet I have ever tasted!

When it comes to tablet, I cannot stand it when it is so heavily crystallized it's like eating a lump of sugar. This should give you a smoother, more palatable eating experience.

MAKES 40 TO 50 SQUARES

1x 14oz (398ml) can condensed milk

5 cups (2lbs) granulated sugar

1 cup plus 2 tablespoons (250g) butter

1x 14oz (398ml) can's worth of whole milk (use the empty condensed milk can to measure)

Few white chocolate buttons or chips

1 cap vinegar

WARNING

This mixture boils at a very high temperature. Be careful.

NOTE

I have found that for one reason or another this recipe doesn't double up to make two batches at the same time. When I need more than one batch, I use the same pot without washing it – any tablet left in the pot really helps to make the next batch cook quicker.

1. Place the condensed milk, sugar, butter and milk into a heavy-bottomed saucepan (wide-based is better).

2. Gently heat until the sugar has dissolved and the butter has melted.

3. Increase the heat until the mixture comes to the boil, stirring the whole time. Keep going until the mixture turns a caramel color; this should take about 20 minutes, but could take longer. The important thing is that you achieve the color and don't forget to keep stirring the whole time.

4. There will be a stage when the mixture starts to boil out of the pan. You will get large rolling bubbles. This is when I remove the pan from the heat and stir until the large bubbles stop coming up.

5. Next, add your chocolate drops and your cap of vinegar.

6. The mixture should start to feel slightly grainy around the sides of the pan at this stage. Please be aware this mix is dangerously hot. Make sure you have the kitchen to yourself and you have plenty of space – as a precaution, I would fill a bowl or sink with water on the off chance you spill some of the mix onto your hands so you are able to cool them instantly. Pour carefully into a 12in x 8in (30cm x 20cm) oiled baking tray.

7. Allow the mix to cool enough that it can be touched without burning your fingers. Whilst it is still soft, you need to cut it into your required shape. Some people use a ruler to obtain perfect squares, but I think it shouldn't be perfect; it should have different sizes. I cut mine free-hand.

8. Allow to fully set. Tablet can be stored in a sealed container for a couple of weeks, but I very much doubt it will last that long.

MILLIONAIRE'S SHORTBREAD

Don't you just love the name millionaire's shortbread? Growing up, I always saw this as a real treat. I understood the name to mean it was so lavish and luxurious and such an upgrade from regular shortbread that you would need to be a millionaire to buy it. Apparently, it's because it is so rich!

This recipe is always a firm favorite with kids who want to start cooking—it's perfect for messy little hands, and the sticky caramel and meted chocolate fascinate them. I remember always looking forward to this being served in the school dinner hall for dessert—partly because it came with custard.

MAKES 8 PORTIONS

For the shortbread

1⅔ cups (250g) all-purpose flour

⅓ cup plus 1 tablespoon (85g) superfine sugar

Scant ¾ cup (170g) butter, softened

For the caramel

2x 14oz (398ml) can condensed milk

For the chocolate topping

7oz (200g) dark or milk chocolate

For the shortbread

1. Heat the oven to 350°F (180°C). Lightly grease and line a 8in x 8in (20cm x 20cm) square baking pan with a lip of at least 1¼in (3cm).

2. To make the shortbread, mix the flour and superfine sugar in a bowl. Rub in the softened butter until the mixture resembles fine breadcrumbs.

3. Knead the mixture together until it forms a dough, then press it into the base of the prepared pan.

4. Prick the shortbread lightly with a fork and bake for 20 minutes or until firm to the touch and very lightly browned. Leave to cool in the pan.

For the caramel

The caramel couldn't be simpler. Take a large pot, fill it with water, place the unopened cans (paper labels removed) into the water and boil for 3 hours. You can also buy the condensed milk pre-caramelized. Once cooked, cool and then spread over the shortbread and leave to cool.

For the chocolate topping

1. Melt the chocolate slowly in a bowl over a pan of hot water. Pour the melted chocolate over the cold caramel and leave to set.

2. To serve, cut into squares or bars with a hot knife.

MACAROON

This delightful little delicacy was invented by the bakers John J. Lees in Coatbridge, near Glasgow, in the 1930s. It is said that he discovered the recipe by accident. If you have a quick scan of the recipe, you will find one ingredient that is rarely found in a sweetie—potato! That's right, this recipe requires the addition of mashed potato. Don't be put off making it though as I think its one of the easiest and best recipes in the book. It is one of those sweets that I loved as a kid; however, if I had known that one of the main ingredients was leftover mashed potatoes I am not sure I would have taken to them so readily.

I made macaroons for the first time about twenty years ago with my son Cameron, as he decided at the age of five he would support his school and set up a sweetie stall at the annual fair. I have been making them ever since and they have graced the tables of the great and the good all around the world as a petit four.

MAKES 4 PORTIONS

2½oz (60g) mashed potato

4½ cups (600g) confectioners' sugar

4oz (125g) quality dark or milk chocolate, melted

4oz (125g) sweetened shredded coconut, toasted and cooled

1. First, make the fondant for the macaroon. To do this, put your mashed potato into a mixer or food processor. Add three-quarters of the confectioners' sugar and slowly mix.

2. Gradually add the confectioners' sugar until you have a dough-type consistency. You might need more sugar – it all depends on how wet your potato is.

3. Next, melt the chocolate in a bowl set over a pan of hot water.

4. Toast your coconut under a medium broiler.

5. Roll out the fondant and cut into bars or whatever shape you prefer.

6. I tend not to dip the cut shapes into the chocolate; I use a pastry brush and carefully coat the fondant with the chocolate. I try and keep the chocolate to a minimum, as it can overpower the other ingredients.

7. Next, as you coat the pieces of fondant in chocolate, drop them into the cooled toasted coconut.

8. Allow the bars to air dry on a cooling rack. Once the chocolate has set, you can store in an airtight container.

BERRY JAM

I just love getting out with my kids and picking blackberries. Where I live in the north of Glasgow we have them growing absolutely everywhere and with the amount we pick making jam is the best way of using them up. We can end up with a year's supply in one day's harvest. When making jam I always use special jam sugar that contains added pectin.

MAKES 3 TO 4 JARS

About 2lbs (900g) blackberries, though you could also use raspberries or strawberries

2lbs 3oz (1kg) jam sugar (or 2lbs 3oz (1kg) granulated sugar mixed with 1/2oz (15g) powdered pectin)

Scant 2 tablespoons (25g) butter

1. Wash your fruit. It is vital that you wash the fruit before cutting the stalks off, especially with strawberries, as they will soak up the water.

2. Once you have allowed the fruit to drip dry, place into a large pan and crush with a potato masher.

3. Next add the sugar and heat it up slowly, stirring the mix continuously.

4. Just before the mix comes to the boil, add the butter.

5. Bring to the boil and then boil for 4 to 5 minutes.

6. To test of it is ready, spoon a little of the mix onto a cold plate; if it is ready, you should see it set up quickly. Run your finger through the puddle on the plate and it should wrinkle. If it stays as a puddle, boil for another couple of minutes.

7. To store, pour the hot jam into sterilized jars.

ORANGE MARMALADE

There has been much debate on the origins of marmalade: some say it was invented in Dundee, others say it has connections to Mary, Queen of Scots. I am not sure who invented it, but it was the Scots who made it a popular breakfast ingredient.

This recipe is from the class notes of Jessie Henderson (whom we met on page 226!), dated the 3rd of June 1893; though the recipe is credited to a Mrs Black.

MAKES 3 TO 4 JARS

About 4lbs (1.8kg) bitter oranges, Seville oranges are perfect for this
5lbs (2.25kg) sugar
2 lemons, juiced
2½ quarts (2½ liters) water

1. Wash and then wipe the oranges with a cloth.

2. Put the whole oranges and lemon juice in a large pan and cover with water.

3. Weigh the oranges down with a plate to keep them submerged.

4. Bring to the boil, cover and simmer very gently for around 2 hours, or until the peel can be easily pierced with a knife.

5. Pour off the cooking liquid from the oranges into a jug and tip the oranges into a bowl.

6. Return the cooking liquid to the pan.

7. Once the oranges have cooled, cut them in half.

8. Scoop out all the pips and pith and add to the cooking liquid. Reserve the peel.

9. Bring the liquid to the boil for 10 minutes.

10. Next, strain this liquid through a sieve into a bowl and press the pulp through with a soup ladle or wooden spoon.

11. Pour the liquid into a pan.

12. Using a sharp knife, cut the peel into fine shreds.

13. Add the peel to the pan with the sugar.

14. Stir over a low heat until all the sugar has dissolved, for about 10 minutes, then bring to the boil and bubble rapidly for 20 to 25 minutes until setting point is reached. You can check this by putting a spoonful of the mix onto a cold plate, allow to stand for a couple of minutes, then push your finger through the puddle of mix; if it wrinkles, the marmalade will set. If not, boil longer until you get it to wrinkle on a cold plate.

15. Take the pan off the heat and skim any scum from the surface.

16. Leave the marmalade to stand in the pan for 20 minutes to cool a little and allow the peel to settle, then pot in sterilized jars.

ELIE NESS LIGHTHOUSE

INDEXES

RECIPE INDEX

LOCATIONS INDEX

ACKNOWLEDGEMENTS

I would like to thank a number of talented producers and suppliers who have supported me in the writing of this book, all of whom I have known and worked with for decades.

Bob Creighton, MBE, has been a true friend and mentor of mine for over 20 years. His dedication to Scotland and North American-Scottish relations is unparalleled. Since the day we met in Chicago in the 90s he has been my anchor, and he has been at the heart of all my North American adventures ever since.

Joe McDougall, Business Development Manager of Alliance Scotland, for supplying the incredible crockery with lots of support from Churchill China, Neville UK and Utopia Tableware.

Stuart Angus, who I have known for almost 30 years, for supplying loads of fruit and vegetables for our cookbook shoot.

Joe Stack from Fresh Select Ltd, a fantastic local butcher company that provided all the butcher meats in the book; he was a brilliant source of advice throughout.

Craig Stevenson of Braehead Foods, another supplier and friend who provided all the game in the book.

Max Johnson and his amazing team of volunteers at the Wash House Garden.

Yvonne Rae and the team at George Campbell & Sons for providing all the incredible fish and shellfish.

And Susie Lowe, for the stunning photography in this book.

ABOUT THE AUTHOR

Born in Glasgow, multi-award-winning chef Gary Maclean has been at the heart of the Scottish hospitality industry for 35 years, working up and down the country to open and develop over 80 venues.

Gary was awarded the title of Scotland's National Chef by the Scottish Government. In this voluntary role, Gary supports the Scottish Government in food health, education and the promotion of Scotland's amazing produce around the world. Gary is an ambassador for Scottish food and food education, and fully believes that every child should be entitled to a quality food education. It is this passion for mentoring young people that led him to become the Executive Chef at City of Glasgow College.

His work in education has been widely recognized: he is a Fellow of the Master Chefs of Great Britain and the International Institute of Hospitality Management, and in 2019 Gary was inducted into the Scotland Colleges Hall of Fame. In 2021 he was also awarded the Mark Twain award by the St Andrews Society of New York for his work on Scottish–American relations. Gary is on the Council of Advisors with the New Hampshire Scots and the Advisory Council of the Saint Andrew's Society of New York State.

In December 2016 he was crowned the champion of BBC's *MasterChef: The Professionals* after taking on 47 other professional chefs in pursuit of gastronomic glory. Since then, Gary has travelled the world to promote Scottish food education and culture, including in the USA, Singapore, India, Indonesia, Malaysia, Colombia, Cuba and Canada.

Gary is the author of *Kitchen Essentials: The Joy of Home Cooking*. He owns a sustainable Scottish seafood restaurant called Creel Caught in the heart of Edinburgh.

UNIVERSITY OF GLASGOW